Text, Photography, and Artwork copyright © 2012 by C&T Publishing

Publisher: Amy Marson

Creative Director: Gailen Runge

Editor: Gailen Runge

Technical Editors: Gailen Runge, Teresa Stroin, and Alison Schmidt

Cover/Book Designer: Kristy Zacharias

Production Coordinator: Jessica Jenkins

Production Editor: S. Michele Fry

Illustrator: Aliza Shalit

Photography by Christina Carty-Francis and Diane Pedersen of C&T Publishing, Inc., unless otherwise noted

Published by Stash Books, an imprint of C&T Publishing, Inc., P.O. Box 1456, Lafayette, CA 94549

Attention Teachers: C&T Publishing, Inc., encourages you to use this book as a text for teaching. Contact us at 800-284-1114 or www.ctpub.com for lesson plans and information about the C&T Creative Troupe.

Library of Congress Cataloging-in-Publication Data

Hat shop : 25 projects to sew, from practical to fascinating / compiled by Susanne Woods.

p. cm.

ISBN 978-1-60705-620-1 (pbk.)

1. Millinery. 2. Hats. I. Woods, Susanne.

TT655.H38 2012

646.5'04--dc23

2011046642

Printed in China

10 9 8 7 6 5 4 3 2 1

Contents

INTRODUCTION

Hats can be functional, hats can be fashionable, and hats can be the finishing touch to the perfect outfit, but there is little doubt that the trend for wearing hats is back. In recent seasons, designers including Marc Jacobs, Proenza Schouler, Carolina Herrera, and Thakoon have featured hats as a major element of their runway collections. But why buy a hat off the rack when you can create a bespoke hat of your own? With this book, we've got you covered.

In compiling this sixth book within our best-selling series of Design Collective titles, I have found fabulous fascinators, practical seasonal hats, fun hats for babies and children, and even some headbands. With 25 projects to choose from, there is something for everyone ... and many are reversible as well. I love the opportunity to experiment with different materials and fabric, add in embellishments and small accessories, or use photo transfer or surface design techniques to make each and every creation unique to the wearer. Most of these hats don't need a lot of fabric to make a big impact and many can be completed in the smaller chunks of time that my (and probably your) busy life allows.

It was my pleasure to have invited a group of incredibly talented designers and milliners to share their fabulous hats or headbands with you. Some of the projects are easily achievable, and some are a bit more of a challenge, but all are sophisticated, original, and stylish designs that I hope you enjoy making and gifting for yourself, friends, and family.

linen fascinator

HAT SIZE: *Fits all*

Make a statement at your next party or wear this along with your Sunday best. Either way, all eyes will be on you with this beautiful, but not overly fussy, headpiece. Embellished with a sweet rosette, this fascinator uses crisp and classic linen for a slightly more casual look. However, if you do get that invitation to the next royal wedding, you can always substitute a taffeta or a silk for the linen.

Katerina Anagnostopoulou is a Greek-based hat designer of Cuban and Czech descent. Her specialties are extravagant custom-made fabric hats; the combination of high design with a touch of vintage glam and excellent craftsmanship is irresistible for most of her customers around the world. As a self-learner, she started her designing career with small projects (aprons and hats) mostly for friends and American philanthropic organizations in Greece. In 2010, after an extremely successful event generated a huge public demand for her items, she decided to turn a fun activity into a small business. With the help of her website, Katerina communicates with her customers and fans fluently in six languages. The best practical present she ever received was a sewing machine.

ARTIST: Katerina Anagnostopoulou
WEBSITE: www.hats.gr

Materials and Supplies

Fabric amounts are based on a 40˝ usable fabric width, unless otherwise noted.

Heavyweight interfacing, ⅛˝ thick*: 1 square 18˝ × 18˝

Linen fabric: 1 rectangle 20˝ × 28˝

Lining: 1 square 8˝ × 8˝ for fascinator base

Light polyester fabric: 1 rectangle 8˝ × 18˝ for flower

1˝-wide bias tape in a matching color: 1 piece 20˝ long

Millinery elastic: 1 piece 13˝ long for headband

*If you don't have ⅛˝-thick interfacing, use 2 layers of thinner interfacing. Simply pin the layers together and continue with the next step of the instructions. Note that you'll need double the amount of interfacing for this method.

Cutting

Template patterns are on pages 14 and 15.

INTERFACING:

Cut 1 base (exterior).

Cut 3 rectangles 6½˝ × 8˝ for the leaves.

LINEN:

Cut 1 base (exterior).

Cut 6 rectangles 6½˝ × 8˝ for the leaves.

LINING:

Cut 1 base (lining).

tip *The best way to cut the base (exterior) from linen is to use the base (exterior) you cut from interfacing instead of the paper pattern. The interfacing is thin and flexible and will make cutting out the shape easier.*

CONSTRUCTION

Fascinator base

1. Place the interfacing for the base on the wrong side of the linen base piece. Pin the interfacing and fabric together and sew all around with a zigzag stitch.

2. Place the 2 B1 points right sides together, and sew from B1 to A1 with a ¼˝ seam allowance. Repeat for the B2 and A2 points. This creates a base for the fascinator's leaves and flower.

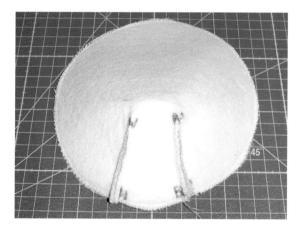

3. Pin the lining to the bottom of the base. Be sure the lining has the same shape as the base and is fully pressed into the center of it before folding the lining fabric at the back of the base. Sew the lining to the base with a zigzag stitch. Trim the excess fabric if necessary.

4. Place the millinery elastic for the headband in the center of each side of the base, against the lining. Sew with a zigzag stitch.

5. Stitch the ends of the bias tape strip together, using a ½˝ seam allowance.

6. Pin the bias tape around the outside edge of the base (exterior), with the right side of the tape against the linen. Center the tape's seam between B1 and B2. Machine stitch ¼˝ away from the edge.

7. Turn the bias to the lining, and pin it. Stitch it to the lining by hand. This adds a nice handmade touch to the fascinator, but make sure your stitches are even!

1. Trace the leaf pattern on all 3 interfacing rectangles.

2. Stack the linen rectangles in pairs with right sides together. Place the interfacing with the leaf pattern on a pair of linen squares, and pin it together to hold it in place. Sew the interfacing onto the fabric along the line you traced, leaving the bottom of the leaf open for turning.

3. Cut out the leaf, leaving approximately ⅛˝ seam allowance. Clip the curves, making sure you don't cut through the seamline.

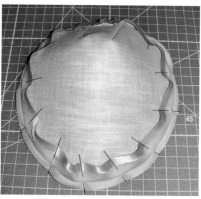

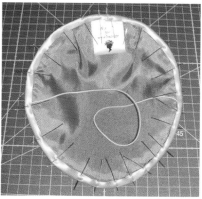

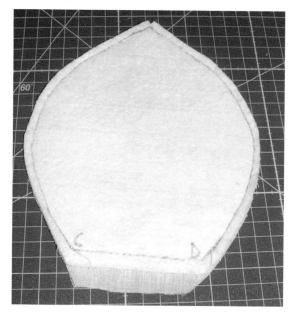

4. Turn the leaf right side out, gently pushing the curves out with the tip of a scissors or pencil to give the proper shape. When the leaf is turned, press it. Don't forget to use a pressing cloth.

5. Fold a pleat, connecting C with D, and pin it. Use a zigzag stitch to sew across the pleat.

7. Repeat Steps 2–6 to finish all 3 leaves. Overlap the bases of the leaves. Pin them, and securely stitch the bases together with a zigzag stitch.

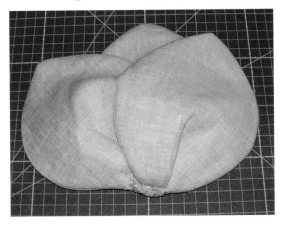

8. Place the leaves on the fascinator base and hand stitch them to the base and each other to stabilize them.

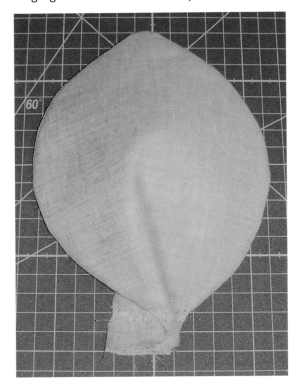

6. Trim the seam allowance below the pleat to ¼˝.

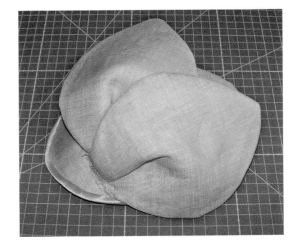

Flower

1. Fold the rectangle of polyester fabric in half lengthwise with wrong sides together. Use a zigzag stitch to sew together the ends and the long edge.

2. Using a needle and a long piece of thread (knotted on the end), baste the edges with the zigzag stitching. Start at a corner and stitch along a short end, along the long edge, and then along the opposite short end. Pull the thread gently to wrinkle the fabric just a bit. Wrap the wrinkled fabric into the shape of a flower. Stitch across the bottom of the flower to secure it.

3. Place the flower on the leaves so that the flower covers the zigzag stitches on the leaves. Hand stitch to secure the flower to the fascinator base and leaves.

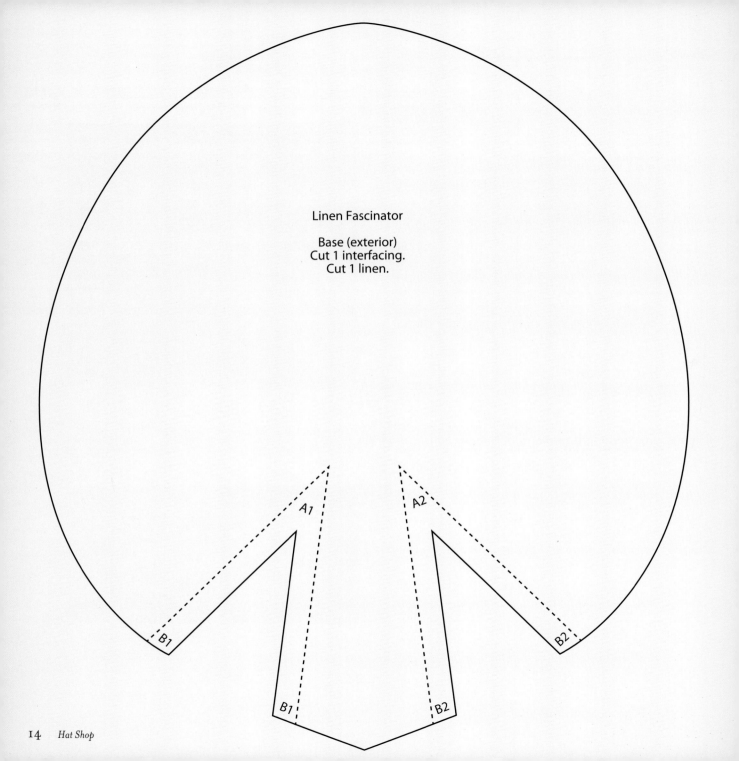

Linen Fascinator

Base (exterior)
Cut 1 interfacing.
Cut 1 linen.

A1 A2

B1 B2

B1 B2

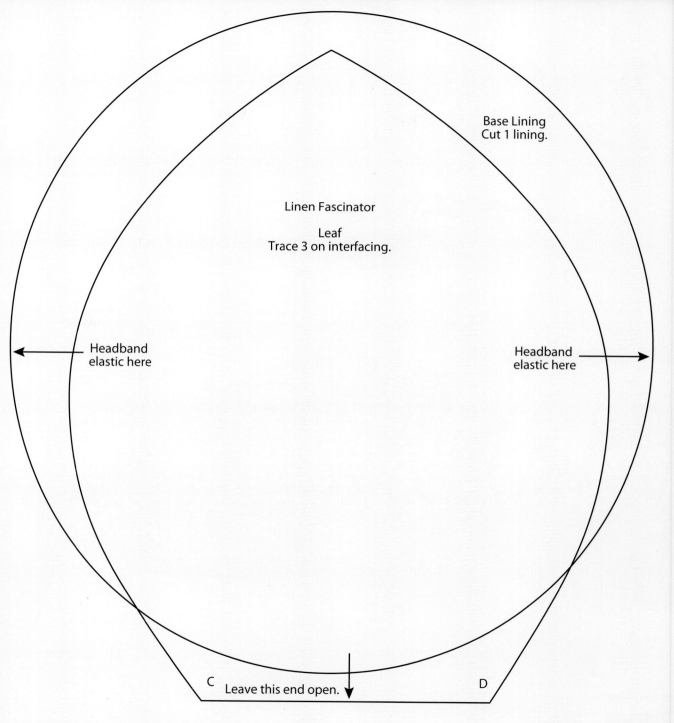

Base Lining
Cut 1 lining.

Linen Fascinator

Leaf
Trace 3 on interfacing.

Headband
elastic here

Headband
elastic here

C Leave this end open. ↓   D

spring sun hat

Constructed from 1½ yards of your favorite quilting-weight cotton and embellished with layers of white linen leaves, this hat is both beautiful and practical. The broad brim protects you from the sun, and you get to look fabulous at the same time. So whether you are spending the morning at your local farmer's market, playing with the kids at the park, or having lunch with friends, this hat makes the everyday a little prettier.

Materials and Supplies

Fabric amounts are based on a 40˝ usable fabric width, unless otherwise noted.

Heavyweight interfacing, 20˝ wide: 2⅛ yards for top, crown, and brim

Cotton or cotton-blend fabric: 1½ yards for hat body

Light polyester lining: ⅜ yard or 1 rectangle 14˝ × 25˝ for lining

Linen fabric: ½ yard or 1 square 25˝ × 25˝ for ribbon and leaves

Grosgrain ribbon: ¾ yard

Cutting

Template patterns are on pullout page P1. Enlarge patterns 200%.

INTERFACING:

Cut 1 top.

Cut 2 brims.

Cut 1 rectangle 3½˝ × 23½˝ for the crown.

COTTON FABRIC:

Cut 1 top.

Cut 2 brims.

Cut 1 rectangle 3½˝ × 23½˝ for the crown.

LINING:

Cut 1 top.

Cut 1 rectangle 3½˝ × 23½˝ for the crown.

LINEN:

Cut 22 leaves.

Cut 1 rectangle 2½˝ × 23½˝ for the ribbon on the crown.

ARTIST: Katerina Anagnostopoulou

WEBSITE: www.hats.gr

For more about Katerina, see her artist's bio (page 9).

CONSTRUCTION

Note: Use a ¼˝ seam allowance unless otherwise noted.

Hat

1. With a zigzag stitch, sew the cotton fabric parts and the interfacing together around the outside edges.

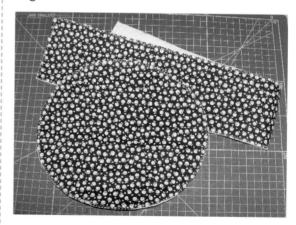

2. Fold a long edge of the linen ribbon under ½" to the wrong side. Pin the wrong side of the ribbon to the right side of the crown piece, aligning the unfolded long edge of the ribbon with the zigzagged bottom edge of the crown.

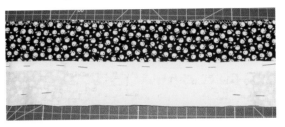

3. Using a straight stitch, topstitch the ribbon to the crown ¼" below the folded top edge. Zigzag stitch the bottom of the ribbon to the bottom edge of the crown.

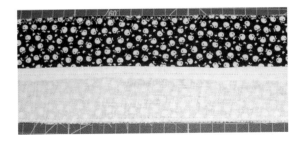

4. With right sides together, sew the short ends of the crown together, forming a ring, and press the seam open.

5. Place the top (interfacing up) on the crown (interfacing out), and pin them right sides together.

6. Sew the top to the crown.

7. Repeat Steps 4–6 with the lining, with right sides together in all the steps.

8. Turn the assembled lining crown upside down, and place it on top of the assembled fabric crown, with the wrong side of the lining top toward the interfacing side of the fabric top.

Be sure to align the seams on the crowns.

9. Use a zigzag stitch to sew the fabric crown and lining crown together around the edge of the top piece.

10. Turn the crown right side out, and shape it.

11. Pin and sew an interfaced brim together at the short ends to create a complete circle.

12. Pin the brim to the crown, with right sides together.

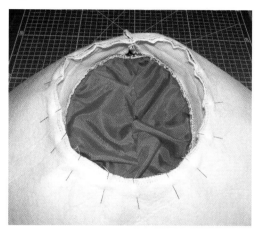

13. With a straight stitch, sew the crown to the brim.

14. Now is the time to check the size. The hat is sized medium to large and fits a head circumference of up to 23˝. The interfacing might make the hat fit a bit more snugly. If this is the case, simply stretch the fabric around the hat gently with your hands. The fabric and interfacing will stretch.

15. Pin and sew the second brim together.

16. Pin the brims together with right sides facing, and sew them along the outside edge.

17. Turn the brim right side out and gently press it. Use steam and a cotton setting, and don't forget to use a pressing cloth.

18. Once again, check the size of the hat. If it seems a bit tight, gently stretch out the fabric.

19. Pin and hand stitch the lining to the brim.

Leaves

20. Measure the hat circumference. Add ½˝ and trim the grosgrain ribbon to this length. Pin the ribbon ends, and sew them together using a ¼˝ seam allowance.

21. Pin the ribbon to the brim and crown lining and stitch it by hand.

1. Cut more leaves if you would like. You can use fewer than the 22 leaves you cut initially if you prefer.

2. Curl the leaves. The best way to curl the leaves is to place them on a soft surface, such as an ironing board. Starting in the middle of a leaf, gently press against the fabric with the dull side of a butter knife while sliding the knife toward the edge of the leaf. It will curl beautifully!

3. Make a fold on the base of each leaf, and pin the ends together.

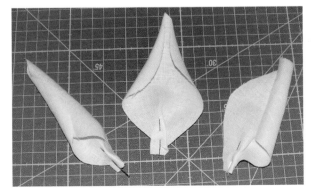

4. Sew the folds either with a zigzag stitch or by hand.

5. Sew the leaves together in pairs, either with a zigzag stitch or by hand.

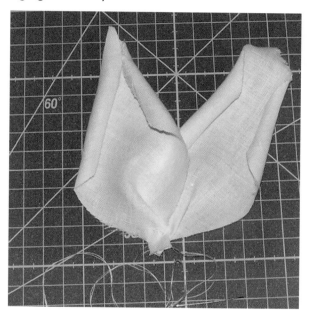

6. Use pins to mark the center front of the hat. Decide where you want to start the leaf cascade. (I placed the center leaves 3˝ to the left of the front center.) With another pin, mark where you want the center of the leaf cascade.

7. Place the leaves in pairs, starting in the middle. Always overlap the leaves as you build the cascade—it's fun! Secure them to the hat with couple of stitches.

1940s half hat

HAT SIZE: *Fits all*

Look like you just stepped off the set of an Agatha Christie film with this fun, perfectly formed half hat. The construction for this one is a little more complicated, but it sure does pay off with a form-fitting, comfortable half hat that is truly a statement piece. Piece together some of your favorite quilting-weight cotton fabrics to create a unique headpiece with vintage flair.

Janine Basil is a milliner and hair accessory designer/maker. Originally from countryside of Devon in the United Kingdom, she is currently settled in the hustle and bustle of good old London. She has a home studio (okay, so it's a spare bedroom!) where she works. She says she's always been a "maker" but started making hats and accessories properly only about 2½ years ago. She specializes in items inspired by burlesque, retro, and geek and never strays far from her quirky British sense of humor!

ARTIST: Janine Basil
WEBSITES: janinebasil.com
janinebasil.etsy.com
facebook.com/JanineBasilHats

Materials and Supplies

Buckram, 20˝ wide: ⅝ yard

Fabrics: 8 strips 2˝–4˝ × width of fabric (strip widths can vary)

Cotton quilt batting: 1 rectangle 8˝ × 15˝

Heavyweight fusible interfacing, 20˝ wide: ¼ yard

Millinery wire: 1 yard

Felt: 1 piece 6˝ × 14˝ for lining and 2 scraps each at least 1˝ × 1˝

Millinery elastic: 2˝

Milliners/straw needle (heavy needle)

1 polystyrene head form (wig stand)

Plastic wrap

Spray bottle and water

Fabric glue

Cutting

From the buckram, cut 2 rectangles on the bias 6˝ × 15˝. The remaining pieces will be cut during the construction process.

CONSTRUCTION

Hat base

1. Cover the polystyrene head with plastic wrap.

2. Spray both buckram pieces lightly with water. Stack them together on top of the head form. Pin a side down below the ear area. The damp buckram pieces should be floppy and pliable. If not, spray them lightly again.

3. Gently pull the loose end of the buckram so it starts to take the shape of the head. Pin it below the opposite ear area.

4. On the top of the head, pin the edges in the middle. Work along the edges, shaping the damp buckram against the head with as few bumps as possible. Pin as needed, working as quickly as you can. If the edges dry, spray them lightly with water, being careful not to saturate the fabric.

5. Leave the buckram to dry for at least 6 hours or preferably overnight.

Fabric top

1. Stitch the strips of fabric together along the long edges with a ¼˝ seam allowance, making 1 large rectangle.

2. Press the seams to the side.

3. Cut a piece 12˝ wide through all the fabric strips. This will be used to cover the hat. Cut a piece of interfacing to fit, and iron it to the wrong side, taking care to keep the seam allowances flat.

4. The remaining fabric will be used later to cut a bias strip for the looped embellishment.

Hat

1. Remove the pins from the hat base. Mark the center point of the buckram on the head form.

2. Measure across the top of your head, from just above each of your ears, and transfer this measurement to the buckram (dividing this number in half and marking from the center point out to each side).

3. Draw a gentle S shape over the top of the buckram using the 3 marks. Draw an outline about 2˝ around the S, creating a shape approximately 4˝ wide. When you are happy with the shape, take the buckram off the form and trim it. You may want to cut outside the line first and try it on, and then make any final adjustments as needed.

4. Using doubled thread, a milliners needle, and a millinery stitch, sew the wire to the underside edges of the hat. Start in the middle of the back, and curve the wire as you go, stitching it around all the edges of the hat. The wire will overlap by approximately 2˝ at the end.

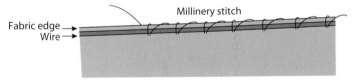

Millinery stitch

5. Spread fabric glue over the top of the hat. Place the batting over it, and ease the batting into shape, ensuring that the hat and batting lie flat with no bumps. Trim the excess batting to within ½˝ of the buckram; notch the curves. Turn the edges of the batting under, and glue them down. Leave the piece to dry for about an hour.

Covering the hat

1. Place the hat back on the head form. Place the 12˝-wide hat fabric piece over the top, on the bias. Pin on the side, under the ear area.

2. Using a steam iron (being very careful not to scald your fingers or melt the head!), ease the fabric tightly over the hat base in the same way as the buckram, pinning as you move around the hat. Allow the fabric to dry.

3. Remove the fabric from the head and cut around the indentation of the hat, leaving at least 2˝ all around.

4. With the hat still on the head, glue the trimmed fabric to the hat as you did with the batting. Leave it to dry.

5. Remove the hat from the head, trim the excess fabric to ½˝, notch the curves, and glue the fabric to the underside.

Embellishing and finishing

1. Cut a bias strip from the remaining fabric, 1½˝ wide and as long as desired. Cut interfacing to match (this does not need to be cut on the bias), and iron it to the wrong side of the fabric.

2. Fold and press under ½˝ along a long edge. Fold the opposite edge to the middle and press. Whipstitch this down by hand, being careful not to let the stitches show on the right side.

3. Have some fun forming loops to your liking, and cut off any excess. Pin the loops to the left side of the hat. Use a milliners needle to stitch them to the hat with small, hidden stitches.

4. Cut 2 squares of felt 1˝ × 1˝. Cut 2 pieces of millinery elastic, each about 1˝ long. Double a piece of the elastic, and wrap some thread around the ends to hold them together. Stitch the elastic to a square of felt with the loop off the edge. Repeat with the other piece of elastic and square of felt. These will be used to bobby pin the hat to your hair.

5. Put the hat on your head again, and adjust the wire if needed to fit comfortably. Decide where you would like the elastic loops. The best place to put them is normally just above the ears, slightly toward the back. The loops should stick out slightly past the edge of the hat.

6. Glue the felt squares to the underside of the hat.

7. Spread glue over the underside of the hat, leaving about ¼˝ around the edges dry. Press the rectangle of lining felt to the underside. Ease it in, and press it down smoothly. Allow the glue to dry. Neatly trim the edges as close to the glue as you can.

reversible baby bonnet

HAT SIZE: *Fits 6-month-old child (head circumference 17˝)*

Make the perfect gift for the new little one in your life. This bonnet is practical and fun. You can select two of your favorite quilting-weight cotton fabrics for this hat as the clever construction technique results in a bonnet that is fully reversible. With its clean lines, this bonnet is suitable for girls or boys and will keep them shaded and cool.

Chio Bloom lives in a 100-year-old Victorian house in Chatham, New Jersey, with her husband, two cheerful boys, a happy goldendoodle named Prince, and a hungry goldfish named King. She grew up in a small coastal town in southern Japan and learned everything she knows about crafts from her mom, Kuniko, in her sunny kitchen. She came to the States to get an MBA but didn't return home after completing her degree because she fell in love with her husband. After many years in finance, Chio decided to stay home with her boys and start an Etsy store, Bloomwoosie. She makes original items for babies, kids, and moms. Everything in her store Chio makes in her little studio "with a lot of love, just like the things I make for my own family," she says.

ARTIST: Chio Bloom, Bloomwoosie
WEBSITES: bloomwoosie.etsy.com
flickr.com/photos/11108386@N07/

Materials and Supplies

Quilting-weight cotton for Fabric A: 1 fat quarter or 1 piece 12″ × 20″

Quilting-weight cotton for Fabric B: 1 fat quarter or 1 piece 12″ × 20″

Light-colored cotton flannel: 1 piece 4″ × 14″ for brim insert

Cotton twill ribbon: ⅞ yard or 2 strips each 15″ long

Round-pointed tool such as Kwik Klip (www.patchworks.com/fingertips.htm)

Cutting

Template patterns are on pullout page P1. Enlarge patterns 200%.

FABRIC A:

Cut 1 side panel.

Cut 1 reverse side panel.

Cut 1 center.

Cut 1 brim on the fold.

FABRIC B:

Cut 1 side panel.

Cut 1 reverse side panel.

Cut 1 center.

Cut 1 brim on the fold.

COTTON FLANNEL:

Cut 1 brim on the fold.

CONSTRUCTION

Note: Use a ¼˝ seam allowance unless otherwise noted.

Brim

1. Place the 3 cut brim pieces (Fabric A, Fabric B, and the flannel) in order as follows: flannel on the bottom, Fabric A next (in the middle) with the right side up, and then Fabric B on top with the wrong side up. Pin them together.

2. Sew ¼˝ from the edge of the outside curve only. Be sure to backstitch at the beginning and end of the seam. Trim the corners. Clip the curves by making small cuts in the seam allowance where the curve is acute.

3. Turn the piece inside out. Now the flannel should be in the middle. Press and topstitch (⅛˝ from the edge) only on the outside curve.

Main bonnet

You will have 2 main bonnets, the first in Fabric A and the other in Fabric B.

1. Place the Fabric A center and the reverse Fabric A side panel right sides together. Make sure that the wider part of the center is at the left. Referring to the labels on the patterns, align the Cr corner on the center with the Cr corner on the reverse side panel. Do the same with the Dr corners. Pin along the curve.

7. Align the brim's inside curve along the brim edge of the Fabric A bonnet, with the center marks matching, and pin them together. Make sure that the Fabric A side of the brim and the right side of the Fabric A bonnet are facing. After pinning, make sure that the distance from the end of the brim to the bottom of the bonnet is the same on both sides. It should be about ½˝.

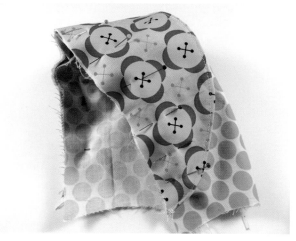

2. Sew the pieces together. Be sure to backstitch at the beginning and end of the seam. Clip the curve.

3. Repeat Steps 1–2 on the other side of the center with the other side panel, aligning the A corner of the center with the A corner of the side panel and the B corners with each other.

4. Turn the bonnet right side out and press the seam allowances toward the center piece.

5. Repeat Steps 1–4 with Fabric B, except press the seam allowances toward the side panels.

6. Fold the brim in half and mark the center on the inside curve. Mark the center of the brim side of the Fabric A bonnet top.

8. Sew the brim and the bonnet together as close as possible to the edge. Make sure the seam allowance is less than ¼˝.

Assembly

1. Pin the cotton twill ribbon onto the Fabric A bonnet along the bottom edge of the bonnet as shown in the photo. Place the ribbon about ¾˝ away from the brim edge. Repeat on the other side with the other ribbon. Fold up the ribbons and secure the folded part onto the middle of the brim with a safety pin to prevent the ribbons from getting caught in the seam as you sew the Fabric A bonnet to the Fabric B bonnet.

2. With the wrong side of the Fabric B bonnet facing out and the right side of the Fabric A bonnet facing out, place the Fabric B bonnet over the Fabric A bonnet with the right sides facing. (The Fabric A bonnet has the brim and the ribbon attached.) Pin them together.

3. Sew along the edge with a ¼˝ seam allowance, leaving a 4˝ opening on the bottom at the back of the neck side. Clip the curve.

4. Turn the bonnet right side out through the opening. Use a round-pointed tool to make sure all the corners are turned cleanly. Remove the pins and the safety pin that were holding the ribbons.

5. Finish the ends of the ribbons by folding in ½˝ twice at the end of each ribbon and stitching.

6. Press the whole bonnet carefully, especially around the brim. Pull back the bonnet part from the brim to make sure no extra fabric is folded in, and then press firmly. Put several pins along the bottom of the brim so that the 2 sides of the bonnet and the brim will not shift when you topstitch. Fold in and close the neck opening with a few pins.

7. Starting at the neck opening, topstitch along the edge of the entire bonnet, ⅛″ from the edge.

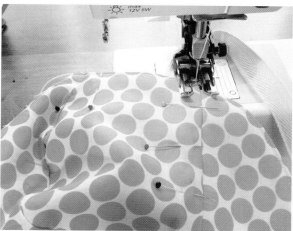

king and
queen for
a day

HAT SIZE: *Adjustable (head circumference up to 24˝)*

A celebratory crown will make anyone feel special. Embellished with sweet felt flowers and customized with the initial of the recipient, this crown is quick and fun to make. Make a bunch of crowns with different embellishments for each guest to wear at a birthday party or other celebration.

Teresa Bright's love of felt began with the idea of a felt party hat. One hat soon grew to more, and her original and custom designs now include crowns, bunting, wands, capes, games and more. She is inspired daily by her twin daughters Stella and Olivia. Teresa specializes in heirloom-quality, one-of-a-kind creations. Her custom designs can be viewed on her blog.

ARTIST: Teresa Bright
WEBSITES: stellandlivi.etsy.com
stellandlivi.wordpress.com

Materials and Supplies

Felt for crown base: 2 pieces 8˝ × 25˝

Felt for oval: 1 piece 2˝ × 2˝

Felt for initial: 1 piece 1½˝ × 1½˝

5 felt colors for flowers: 1˝ × 12˝ strips of each color

Fusible web: 1 piece 8˝ × 28˝

Hook and loop fastener: 3˝-long piece

Embroidery floss

Initial pattern approximately 1˝ × 1˝ in desired font

Swarovski crystals for embellishment (optional)

Craft glue

Cutting

Template patterns are on pullout page P2. Enlarge patterns 200%. Apply fusible web to the back of a piece of crown base felt, the oval felt, and the initial felt before cutting. Create your own initial pattern by enlarging a font on a computer to approximately 1˝ high.

FELT FOR CROWN BASE WITH FUSIBLE APPLIED:
Cut 1 crown base.

FELT FOR OVAL:
Cut 1 oval.

FELT FOR INITIAL:
Cut 1 initial.

FELT FOR FLOWERS:
Cut 40 petals.

CONSTRUCTION

Crown base

1. Sew the hook side of the hook and loop fastener to the front right end of the crown, leaving a ½˝ space at the end of the crown base.

2. Iron the cut-out crown base onto the second 8˝ × 25˝ piece of felt. Trim around the attached crown to remove excess felt.

3. Sew the opposite (loop) side of the hook and loop fastener onto the back side of the left end of the crown.

4. Using embroidery floss, sew around the entire outside edge of the crown with a blanket stitch.

Initial

1. Fuse the initial to the oval.

2. Blanket stitch around the oval.

3. Fuse the oval to the center front of the crown.

Creating the flowers

1. Place a petal across another to look like an X.

2. Using a needle and floss, sew the centers of the 2 petals together. Squeeze slightly to create a dimple in the center.

3. Repeat Steps 1 and 2 to create 20 flowers in the variety of selected felt colors.

Attaching the flowers

1. Apply a dab of craft glue to the back center of a flower.

2. Attach the flower to the crown in the desired location. Hold the flower in place until the glue adheres to the crown.

3. Repeat Steps 1 and 2 until all the flowers are applied.

4. *Optional:* Apply crystal embellishments to the centers of the flowers using craft glue.

little red riding hat

HAT SIZE: *Medium*

Red Riding Hood all grown up! Inspired by 1920s styling, this sweet and stylish designer hat is simply constructed from 3mm-thick felt. With the addition of just a few feathers, this hat is transformed into a sassy little update on the classic riding hat that is minimalist in construction but still makes a big impact.

Anna Cavaliere grew up and lives in Italy. She works at the Teatro Sociale di Como, directing the costume department. Fascinated by fashion history, she first started making hats to celebrate the elegance and style of the 1920s, and soon, after discovering new shapes and materials, it was too late to stop. Her original patterns mix a whimsical retro style with a contemporary and minimalist irony reflected in neat lines and brilliant solid colors.

ARTIST: Anna Cavaliere, RetroReproHandmade
WEBSITE: retroreprohandmade.etsy.com

Materials and Supplies

Red felt, 3mm thick, 36˝ wide: ⅜ yard or 1 rectangle 15˝ × 30˝

2 (or more) red goose biot feathers

Cutting

Template patterns are on pages 40–43. Enlarge Brim pattern 200%.

RED FELT:

Cut 1 crown front (A), 1 crown side (B), 1 crown back (C), 1 crown side (D), and 1 brim (E). No seam allowance is required.

Cut 1 strip ⅜˝ × 20˝ for the spiral embellishment.

CONSTRUCTION

1. Lay pieces A and B next to each other. Do not overlap the 2 pieces of felt. Use a zigzag stitch (medium length) to sew the 2 pieces together, guiding them under the machine foot from the f corner on A and the i corner on B down to the g and m corners. Refer to the pattern pieces for the corner designations. Pull the felt a bit with your hands while sewing. This side of the hat will have a natural curved shape once sewn.

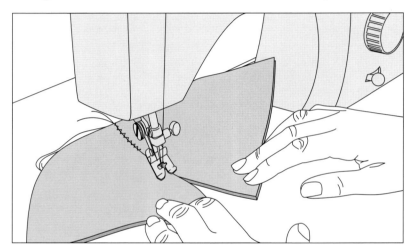

2. Repeat Step 1 with the C and D pieces, butting the edges together again and sewing from the n and q corners to the o and s corners. At the same time, pull the felt a bit with your hands. The seams will give a curved shape to each side of the hat.

3. Again, use a zigzag stitch (medium length) and abut the edges to sew together AB and CD, from the top point where the 4 corners (f, i, n, and q) meet down to corners r and h. You can pull the felt a bit with your hands while machine sewing to make the seam meet tightly.

4. Repeat Step 3 to sew the last seam of AB and CD together, starting at the top where the 4 corners meet and matching corner p to corner l.

5. Sew the brim (piece E) to the bottom of the hat, starting from point w (on D) and matching it to point t (on E). Sew with a zigzag stitch, butting the edges together, to pieces A, B, and C until the brim is completely stitched in place. The brim is cut smaller than the circumference of the hat, allowing space for embellishments.

6. Twist the ⅜˝ × 20˝ felt strip into the shape of a spiral around your fingers (making varied sizes of loops). Hand stitch the strip to the hat where desired.

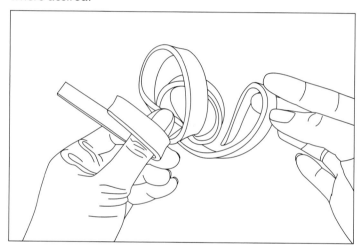

7. Add 2 or more goose biot feathers, or different feathers, hand stitching them to the hat with a hidden stitch behind the spiral embellishment.

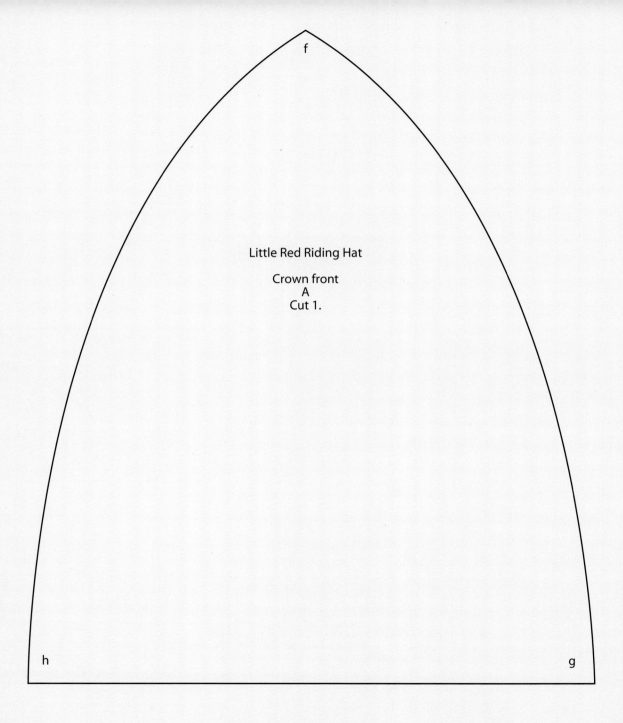

f

Little Red Riding Hat

Crown front
A
Cut 1.

h

g

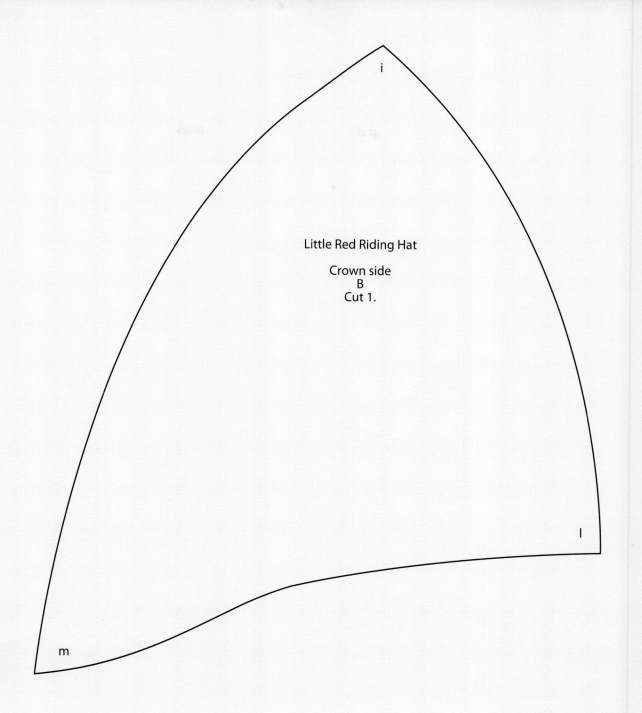

i

Little Red Riding Hat

Crown side
B
Cut 1.

l

m

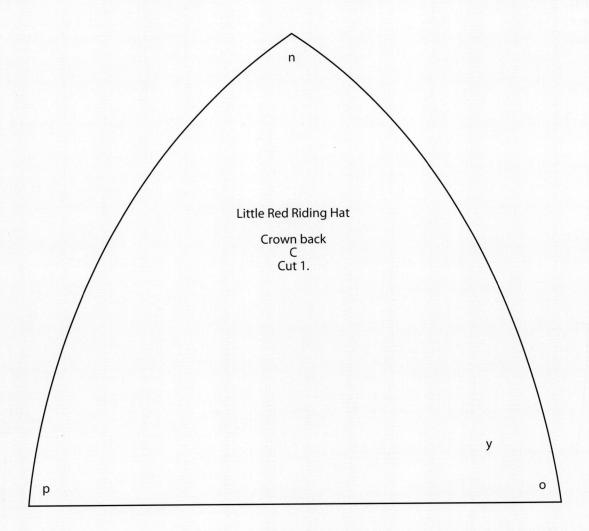

Little Red Riding Hat

Crown back
C
Cut 1.

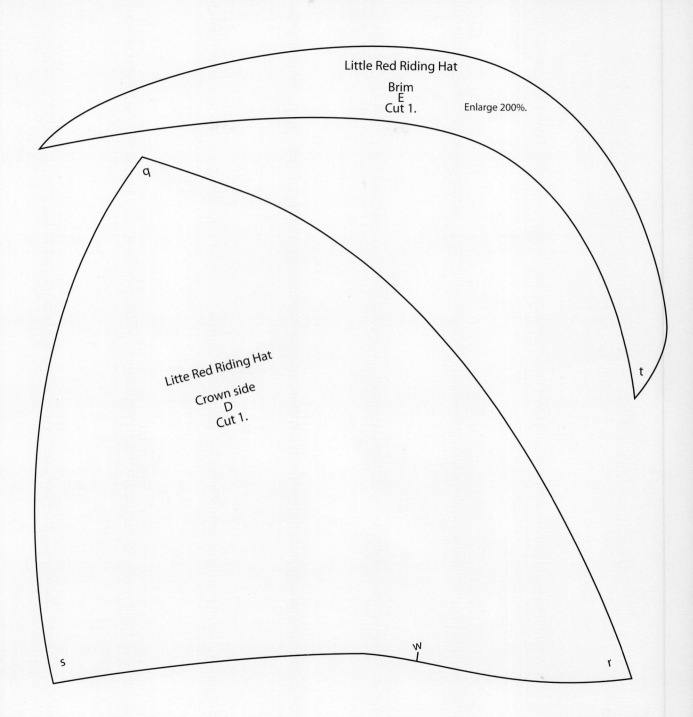

Little Red Riding Hat

Brim
E
Cut 1.

Enlarge 200%.

q

t

Litte Red Riding Hat

Crown side
D
Cut 1.

s

w

r

cappuccino bowler

HAT SIZE: *Medium*

This hat is a new twist on a classic bowler, with a broad brim in the front and a tidy bow as a subtle accent. Constructed from 3mm-thick felt, this hat is all about clean lines and accurate sewing. Because of the minimal construction, spending your time getting the pattern pieces right will pay off in a fabulous fit

ARTIST: Anna Cavaliere, RetroReproHandmade

WEBSITE: retroreprohandmade.etsy.com

For more about Anna, see her artist's bio (page 37).

Materials and Supplies

Beige felt, 3mm thick: 1 rectangle 15˝ × 30˝

Black felt: 1 strip ⅓˝ × 14˝ (can be replaced with black ribbon)

4 teal sequins

3 black sequins

Cutting

Template patterns are on pullout page P1. Enlarge patterns 200%.

BEIGE FELT:

Cut 1 each of the top (A) and brim (C). No seam allowance is required.
Cut 1 strip 3⅛˝ × 24½˝ for the crown.
Cut 1 strip 1˝ × 7˝ for a bow.

CONSTRUCTION

1. To sew the 3⅛˝ × 24½˝ rectangle for the crown to the top (template A), lay the 2 pieces next to each other. Do not overlap them. Use a zigzag stitch (medium length) to sew the 2 pieces together, guiding them under the machine foot, matching a corner of the crown to the d mark on A. Stich around the circumference of A, and overlap the 2 ends of the crown ½˝ or so.

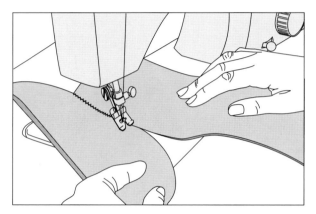

2. Adjust the overlap of the corners at the lower edge of the crown to customize the hat to the size needed. Place a few tiny stitches at the overlap to secure.

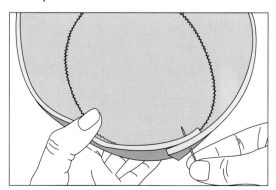

3. Again using a zigzag stitch and butting the edges together, sew the brim (template C) to the lower edge of the crown, placing corner i (on the brim) about 5″ toward the front left of the back seam of the crown. The back (seam) side of the hat has no brim and will feature the embellishment.

4. Stitch the black felt strip (or black ribbon) by hand over the seam between the brim and the crown, leaving the last 2″ of the black strip unsewn at point l and hanging past the angled end of the brim.

5. Turn the brim up to the side of the crown at point q and hand stitch it in place with an invisible stitch to keep it upward on that side. Sew a teal sequin onto the same point q.

6. Embellish the brim by hand stitching 1 teal and 2 black sequins as indicated by the stars on the template.

7. Hand stitch the short edges of the beige strip together as if to make a bracelet. Pinch the circle together in the middle to look like a figure 8 or a bow, and stitch through the center.

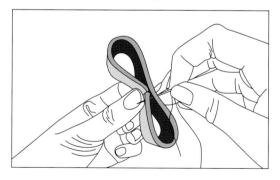

8. Place the bow on a slight diagonal on the back of the crown and hand stitch it in place. Then sew the remaining sequins in the middle of the bow.

9. Put on the hat, and shape the brim with your hand, giving it a fluid and neat slope.

daisy and dots headband

SIZE: *Fits baby through adult**

This pretty little headband is great for girls of all ages with a wide cut and a cute yo-yo flower embellishment. This is the perfect project for using some of your scraps and so fast and easy to make that you can match one to every outfit! The elastic at the back is enclosed in a fabric casing so that it will be comfortable and easy to wear. If you leave off the flower embellishment, this headband can be reversible— effectively making two headbands in one!

Anthea Christian has been creating and crafting for as long as she can remember. As a child she made her own Barbie doll clothes and dollhouse furnishings. Since then she has honed her skills through years of experience at the sewing machine, sewing clothing for herself and her children and items for the home. In 2008 she began selling her creations online, under the label Angel Lea Designs. She soon discovered that her passion lay in the design process rather than the repetitive sewing of items, so she decided to launch her own line of patterns. She designs a range of fresh and fun patterns for children's clothing, soft toys, bags, appliqué designs, and anything else that strikes her fancy. Her patterns are easy to follow and include detailed step-by-step instructions, which are backed up by photographs, making them achievable for even the confident beginner.

ARTIST: Anthea Christian
Angel Lea Designs
WEBSITE: angelleadesigns.com

*SIZE: *Headband measures 2⅛˝ wide at widest point for all sizes; see size chart below for circumferences.*

SIZE CHART

Size	Fits head circumference	Age
Small	17˝–19˝	6–12 months
Medium	18½˝–20½˝	1–3 years
Large	19¾˝–21⅝˝	4–7 years
Extra large	21˝–23˝	8 years–adult

Materials and Supplies

Orange dot cotton fabric: ⅜ yard for headband and small yo-yo

Contrast stripe cotton fabric: ¼ yard for large yo-yo and button covering

¾˝-wide elastic: 1 piece 6½˝ long

⅞˝ self-cover button

Bodkin or safety pin

Tweezers

Hot glue gun (optional)

Cutting

Template patterns are on pages 52 and 53.

ORANGE DOT FABRIC:

Cut 2 headbands.

Cut 2 elastic casings.

Cut 1 small yo-yo circle, 4⅝˝ diameter.

CONTRAST STRIPE FABRIC:

Cut 1 large yo-yo circle, 6⅛˝ diameter.

Cut 1 button cover circle, 1½˝ diameter.

CONSTRUCTION

Note: Use a ¼˝ seam allowance unless otherwise noted.

Headband

1. Fold back each end of both of the curved headband pieces ⅝˝ to the wrong side of the fabric and press. Stitch the 2 headband pieces right sides together along both curved sides. Leave the ends open.

2. Stitch the elastic casing pieces right sides together along both long sides. Leave the ends open.

3. Clip the curves on the headband, and then turn both pieces right side out. Press.

4. Insert the 6½˝ length of elastic into the casing, using a bodkin or safety pin, and thread it through until the end of the elastic reaches the other end of the casing. Stitch across the end of the casing to secure the elastic in place, and remove the safety pin or bodkin.

5. Pull the opposite end of the elastic back out until it reaches the unstitched end of the casing. Stitch across the end of the casing to secure the elastic in place.

6. With the help of a pair of tweezers, insert an end of the casing ½˝ inside an open end of the headband. Topstitch the end of the headband in a rectangular shape to secure the casing inside.

7. Repeat Step 6 with the other end of the casing and the other open end of the headband.

8. If desired, topstitch the curved edges of the headband ⅛˝ from the edge of the fabric.

Yo-yo flower

1. Fold the edge of the large yo-yo circle over ¼˝ to the wrong side of the fabric to form a hem, and then hand stitch around the circumference of the circle using small, even running stitches ¼˝ in length and ¼˝ apart. When you get back to the starting point, pull on the thread to gather the fabric up into the center. Tie off the thread to secure the gathers.

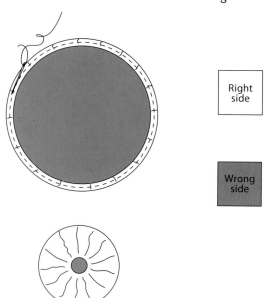

Right side

Wrong side

2. Repeat with the small yo-yo circle.

3. Cover the self-cover button with the prepared fabric circle, following the package instructions.

4. Place the small yo-yo on top of the large yo-yo and stitch through the center of both to hold them together. Stitch the self-covered button onto the center of the small yo-yo.

5. To determine the placement of the yo-yo flower on the headband, fold the headband in half and place the edge of the flower even with the center fold of the headband.

6. Stitch the yo-yo flower to the headband in 2 or more places, working from the back of the headband.

7. If you are making the headband for a young child, it is a good idea to also glue the button and yo-yos in place using a hot glue gun to make sure they are secure.

tip *To make a reversible headband, leave off the yo-yo flower, and use a different fabric for each side. Alternatively, attach the yo-yo flower to a brooch pin back so that it is removable.*

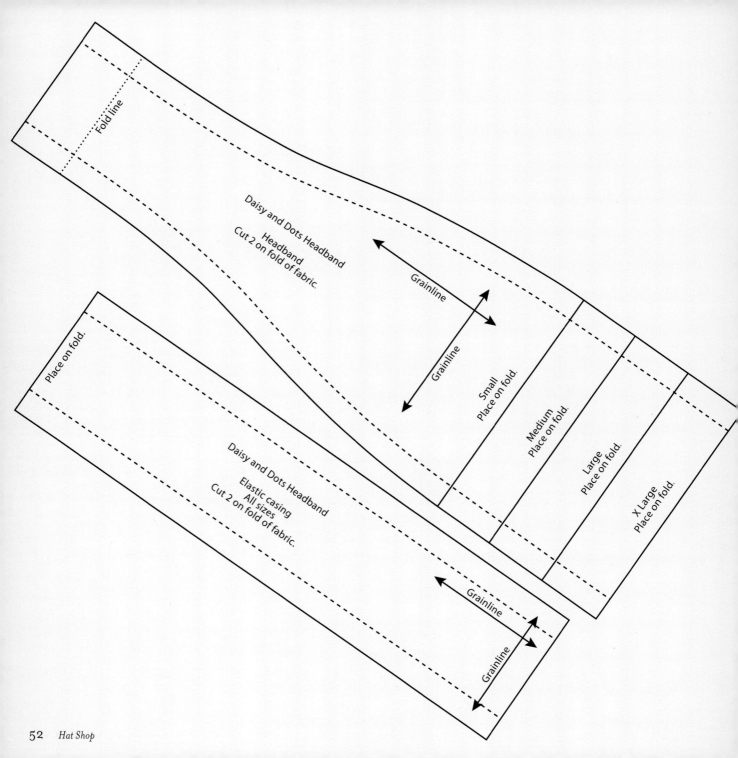

Fold line

Daisy and Dots Headband
Headband
Cut 2 on fold of fabric.

Grainline

Grainline

Small
Place on fold.

Medium
Place on fold.

Large
Place on fold.

X Large
Place on fold.

Place on fold.

Daisy and Dots Headband
Elastic casing
All sizes
Cut 2 on fold of fabric.

Grainline

Grainline

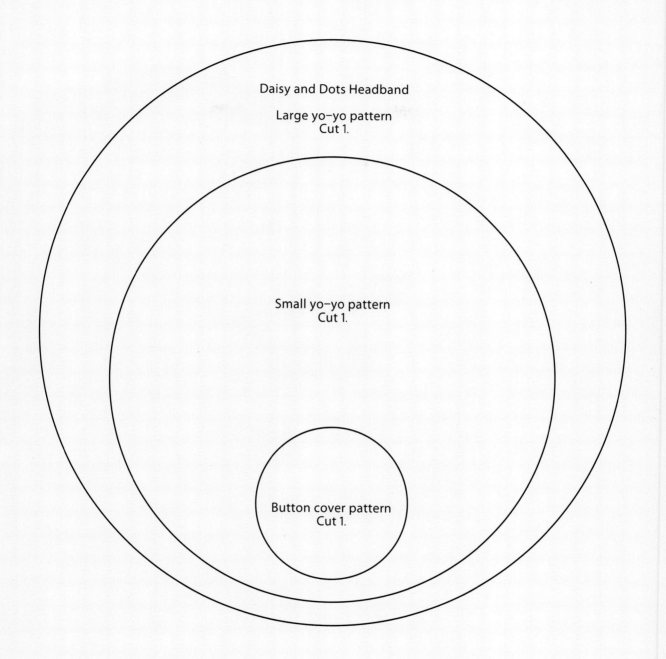

Daisy and Dots Headband

Large yo–yo pattern
Cut 1.

Small yo–yo pattern
Cut 1.

Button cover pattern
Cut 1.

tie-back sun visor

HAT SIZE: *Fits all*

Look like you just stepped off the tennis court with this flirty visor that also acts as a headband. This design shows that sometimes the simplest concepts are the most beautiful and useful. It's easy to store or pack, and it's great to have on hand when traveling. This carefree visor is a simple project with a vintage touch.

Australian crafter *Christen Dell* began twirling betty (named for her grandmother's romantic tales of being twirled around the dance floor by Christen's grandfather) when she couldn't find hair accessories she liked to control her daughter's crazy toddler hair! Two years and another daughter later, twirling betty now sells a range of handmade fabric products, from Christen's signature tie-back sun visors to fabric cake decorations. On her blog, Christen shares tutorials for inspiring projects and her quest to cook and grow things for her family. It also provides a glimpse into her sometimes chaotic life with two little girls who twirl constantly.

ARTIST: Christen Dell, twirling betty
WEBSITES: twirlingbetty.com.au
twirlingbetty.wordpress.com
twirlingbetty.etsy.com (USD)
madeit.com.au/twirlingbetty (AUD)
twitter.com/twirlingbetty
facebook.com/twirlingbetty
pinterest.com/twirlingbetty

Materials and Supplies

Fabric (at least 44˝ from selvage to selvage):
⅓ yard for visor brim and headband

Medium-weight nonwoven interfacing: 1 rectangle 4˝ × 10˝

Cutting

Template pattern is on pullout page P1. Enlarge pattern 200%.

FABRIC:

Cut 2 brims.

Cut 2 rectangles 2½˝ × 44˝ for the headband piece.

INTERFACING:

Cut 1 brim.

CONSTRUCTION

Note: Use a ⅛˝ seam allowance unless otherwise noted.

Constructing the brim

1. Place the fabric brim pieces right sides together.

2. Lay the interfacing piece on top, and pin the 3 pieces together.

3. Beginning roughly halfway along the straight edge, sew all the way around the brim piece, leaving an opening of about 2˝ through which to turn the piece right side out. Clip the curves.

4. Turn the brim right side out. You will be left with a brim piece that has the interfacing sewn in between the fabric layers.

Joining the headband and brim

1. Place the headband strips right sides together, and lay them horizontally in front of you.

2. Mark the center point on the top edge (farthest away from you) of the top piece of headband fabric.

3. Mark the center point on the top edge of the bottom piece of headband fabric. (The mark will be on the wrong side of the fabric on the uppermost headband strip and on the right side of the fabric on the bottom headband strip.)

4. Mark the center point on the straight edge of the brim piece.

5. Sandwich the brim piece between the top and bottom headband strips and align the 3 center marks so that the center of the brim is aligned with the centers of both headband strips. Note: For now, the rounded part of the brim piece will extend beyond the bottom edge of the headband strips.

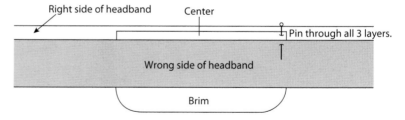

6. Pin in place along the straight edge through all the layers.

Assembling the visor

1. Starting from the previously marked center points, measure approximately 12˝ to the right. Begin sewing from this point toward the brim.

2. Continue sewing around the edges, pivoting at the corners, until you reach the point on the opposite edge where the rounded part of the brim piece extends out beyond the headband strips.

3. Carefully fold or roll the brim piece inward so that you can continue sewing the headband strips together. Take great care to ensure that the brim piece is pushed sufficiently in from where you will continue sewing so that it is not caught up as you sew.

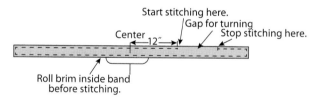

Start stitching here.
Gap for turning
Center
Stop stitching here.
12˝
Roll brim inside band before stitching.

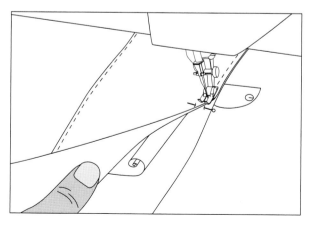

4. Continue sewing all the edges, leaving a 5˝ gap for turning. You will be left with a rectangular tube with the brim piece sewn inside it.

5. Trim the excess fabric on each corner to allow for a cleaner point when the piece is turned right side out.

6. Turn the visor right side out and use a dull pointed instrument (I use a wooden chopstick) to poke out the corners crisply.

7. Iron the visor, folding in the edges at the turning gap so that they align with the sewn edges.

8. Topstitch the headband, closing the turning gap in the process.

9. Topstitch the curved edge of the brim.

10. Pop it on your head, tie it in the back, and start twirling!

kid's flat cap

HAT SIZE: *Head circumference 18½˝, 19¼˝, or 20¼˝*

Handsome. Dapper. Sporty. Yes, all of these. This fresh take on the newsboy is designed with a low-profile fit and a smooth, finished back. A modern Echino print in cotton/linen paired with the dashing shimmer-dot brim gives this classic look currency. Finished inside with a crisp organic-cotton poplin, the cap offers a smooth and comfortable fit as well as a design that will wear well from one season to the next. And with no exposed seams to distract or fray, it can be lovingly handed down from one child to another.

A goldsmith by trade, *Dory Smith Graham* is a self-taught textile designer with a focus on accessories, incorporating both utility and modern detail. Her creative streak got about a mile wide with the birth of her son. In 2008 she launched worthygoods with several sporty hat patterns designed for her new little guy. Pattern making allows her inner designer room to play, while a textile medium satisfies her senses. Recently, worthygoods expanded to include worthygoods textile, an organic textile shop that includes many of the sustainable fabrics used in her worthygoods accessories. Dory lives on an island off the coast of Maine with her always-encouraging husband and their young son and new daughter. Inspiration is found while out adventuring in the gorgeous combinations of weather and landscape that Maine offers.

ARTIST: Dory Smith Graham, worthygoods

WEBSITES: worthygoods.etsy.com (handmade accessories) worthygoodstextile.etsy.com (organic textiles)

Materials and Supplies

Cotton/linen print: ½ yard for body of hat and brim

Fusible interfacing, tailor-weight, 20˝ wide: 1 yard for body

Cotton poplin fabric: ½ yard for lining

Bright accent fabric: 1 scrap 8˝ × 10˝ for brim

Heavy nonfusible interfacing: ⅓ yard for brim

tips

When selecting fabrics for the hat itself, here are a few things to consider:

- *You will want something with a bit of body, heavier than a typical quilting cotton, for the outer layer. The cotton/linen blend shown results in a crisp-looking hat that wears well and spot washes nicely.*

- *Tropical wool is a wonderful weight for a fall, winter, and early spring look. Tartans are the real classic when it comes to a flat cap. To keep a modern edge, you'll want to pay special attention to the contrasting brim fabric.*

- *Pinwale corduroy is light enough and has excellent body. You may omit the interfacing when using this type of fabric because it has enough structure on its own. Also, a heavy hand with an iron when fusing the interfacing may disturb the nap.*

Cutting

Template patterns are on pullout page P2. Enlarge patterns 200%. Seam allowances are included in the template patterns. Before cutting, fuse the interfacing to the wrong side of the cotton/linen fabric.

COTTON/LINEN WITH FUSIBLE ATTACHED:

Cut 1 body.

Cut 1 brim.

Cut 1 crown.

COTTON POPLIN:

Cut 1 body.

Cut 1 crown.

BRIGHT ACCENT FABRIC:

Cut 1 brim.

HEAVY INTERFACING:

Cut 1 brim.

CONSTRUCTION

Note: For all the steps, secure the seams with a backstitch at the start and finish, and use a ½″ seam allowance unless otherwise noted.

1. Sandwich the brim pieces together, with the interfacing on the outside and the cotton/linen and bright accent fabrics right sides together. Pin around the outside edge. Starting at a corner, stitch around the pinned edge of the brim. Turn the brim right side out, and press the seam flat.

2. Topstitch along the outside edge. Topstitch around the brim again, using the last stitch line to maintain the seam allowance. Repeat once more. Set aside.

3. Place the cotton/linen body and crown pieces right sides together, match the centers (fold line), and pin the outside corners of the crown to the body; then pin around the curve. Repeat with the cotton poplin crown and body pieces.

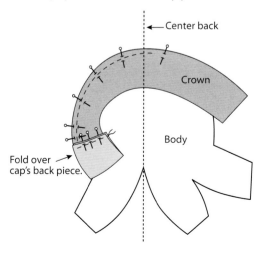

Center back

Crown

Body

Fold over cap's back piece.

4. Sew along the pinned edge of the body and crown for the cotton/linen pieces and the cotton poplin pieces. At each inside corner, carefully raise your sewing machine's presser foot, turn the fabric, and lower the foot to stitch again. This will keep a neat finished look.

5. Pin each of the 3 back seams of the body for both the cotton/linen and the cotton poplin pieces. Sew along each pinned edge. These joined body and crown sections are the hat body.

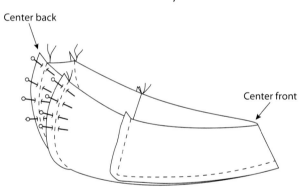

Center back

Center front

6. Turn the cotton/linen hat body right side out, and find the centers of both the crown part of the hat body and the finished brim at their raw edges. Match the centers, with the bright accent side of the brim facing the right side of the cotton/linen crown, and pin. Continue pinning the crown to the brim along the inside curve of the brim.

7. Tuck the cotton/linen hat body, pinned to the brim, into the cotton poplin lining hat body (still right side in); the right sides will be together as shown. Line up all the centers and seams, and match and pin the seams; repin the brim as well between the raw edges of both hat bodies. Starting at a side back hat body seam, sew around the pinned edge, moving around the front of the hat and ending at the other side back seam. The opening left at the back of the hat is for turning.

8. Turn the hat right side out through the opening at the back. Push the lining smoothly inside the cotton-lined hat with your hands. Press the seam flat from one corner of the brim to the other corner. Press under the raw edges at the opening in the back, and pin closed at the center seam. Sew along the outside edge you just pressed. Again, starting at a corner of the brim, stitch around the back of the hat to the other edge of the brim. This encloses the opening in the back and provides stability. Closely clip any stray threads.

9. *Optional:* With a sewing needle and thread, tack the very center of the outer brim seam to the center cotton/linen crown with a few stitches. Tacking the brim down completes the overall look, but leaving it open allows the crown to pop up for more of an engineer-type look. Experiment and find what look you like best.

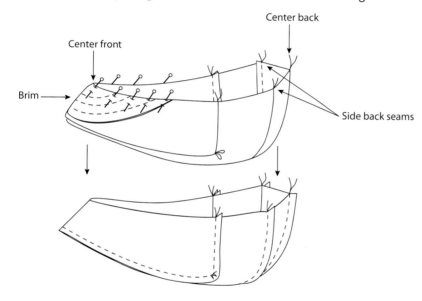

Center back

Center front

Brim

Side back seams

winter flap

HAT SIZE: *Women's and men's medium*
(head circumference 22½˝ and 24˝)

Lookin' good in the winter wonderland neighborhood! This winter hat is gender neutral; it manages to look handsome for the guys and and smart for the girls. And it can even handle a low-tied ponytail (for the girls or guys). This hat easily transitions from fall to winter, so when the weather begins to get cold and windy, just turn down the flap to keep your ears and neck warm and cozy.

Materials and Supplies

Wool tartan, suiting-weight: ½ yard for shell

Fleece: ½ yard for lining

Heavyweight sew-in interfacing: 1 piece 5˝ × 9˝ for brim stiffening

Matching button, 1˝ diameter

When selecting fabrics for the hat itself, here are a few things to consider:

- *Tropical-weight wool is a wonderful weight for fall and winter. A heavier-weight wool will result in a slightly stiffer but warmer cap overall.*
- *Pinwale corduroy is light enough and has excelent body, though it is not as warm.*
- *Consider clean, unused (new) vintage fabric as well as upcycling a gently used old throw or skirt.*
- *A leather-wrapped or wooden button can be just the right touch for this hat.*

tips

Cutting

Template patterns are on pullout page P2. Enlarge patterns 200%.

WOOL TARTAN:	FLEECE:	HEAVY INTERFACING:
Cut 6 crowns.	Cut 6 crowns.	Cut 1 brim.
Cut 1 brim.	Cut 1 brim.	
Cut 1 earflap.	Cut 1 earflap.	

ARTIST: Dory Smith Graham, worthygoods
WEBSITE: worthygoods.etsy.com
(handmade accessories)
worthygoodstextile.etsy.com
(organic textiles)
*For more about Dory, see her artist's bio
(page 59).*

CONSTRUCTION

Note: Use a ½˝ seam allowance unless otherwise noted, and always secure the seams with a backstitch at the start and finish. When pressing, use a warm iron with no steam.

Brim and earflap

1. Sandwich the brim pieces, placing the wool tartan and fleece right sides together and the interfacing on the outside. Pin around the outside edge. Sew the pinned edge. Turn the brim right side out and lightly press the seam flat.

2. Topstitch along the outside edge of the brim, following the curve. Topstitch 2 additional rows, each ½˝ away from the previous line of stitching. Set aside the finished brim.

3. Pin the earflap wool tartan and fleece pieces right sides together. Stitch around the entire length of the outside curved edge, leaving the long straight side open for turning. Turn the earflap right side out, and lightly press the seam flat. Topstitch along the pressed seam for additional stability and structure. Set aside.

Crown

When sewing the crown seams, use a ⅝˝ seam allowance for the women's size. For the men's size, use a ⅜˝ seam allowance.

1. Align 3 pairs of wool tartan crown pieces, and pin each pair right sides together. Sew a side of each pair from the bottom to the dot at the top of the pattern, backstitching at the end of each seam.

2. Open 2 sewn pairs, align them with right sides together, matching the top edges, and stitch them together along one edge.

3. Repeat Step 2 with the third crown section. Now all the sections have been joined.

4. To complete the crown, align the outer edges with right sides together, matching the edges at the top, and stitch the final seam.

5. Trim ⅓˝ off the seam allowances from the top of each crown seam. Press the seams flat.

6. Repeat Steps 1–5 with the 6 crown pieces in fleece, but do not press the seams.

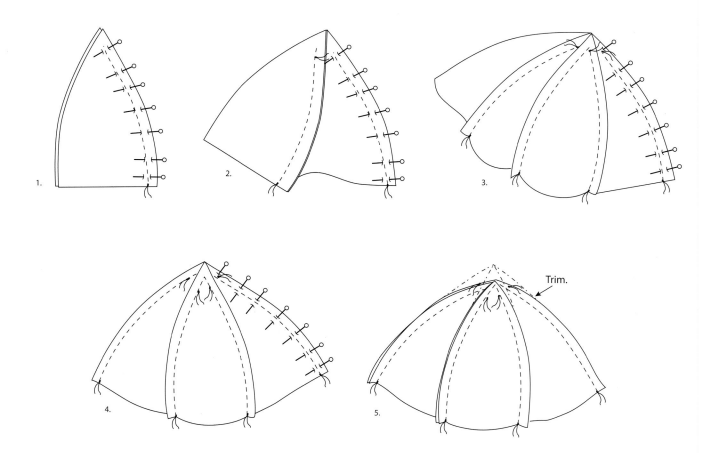

1.

2.

3.

4.

5.

Trim.

Assembly

1. Turn the wool tartan crown right side out and upside down. Match a crown seam to the center of the brim, with the right sides of the wool tartan together and raw edges aligned; pin along the curve of the brim.

2. Pin the center of the earflap to the crown seam opposite the center of the brim, with the right sides of the wool tartan together and raw edges aligned.

3. Pin the earflap around the crown, making sure the spaces between the earflap and the brim are even. The men's size will have a bit more space between the earflap and the brim edges than the women's size.

4. With the fleece crown wrong side out and upside down, place the wool tartan crown/brim/earflap into the fleece crown, with right sides together. Match the crown seams and pin.

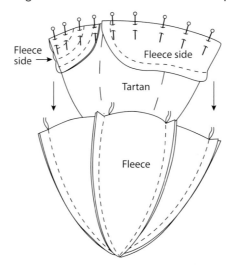

Fleece side

Fleece side

Tartan

Fleece

5. Starting at a side back crown seam, sew around the front of the hat using a ½˝ seam allowance; end at the other side back crown seam, leaving an opening for turning.

6. Turn the hat right side out through the opening. When turning the hat, be sure to keep the earflap against the tartan crown; pin it in place on the right side. Smooth the fleece lining inside the wool tartan hat with your hands. Pull the earflap down, and lightly press the seam around the entire hat. Turn under the raw edges of the wool opening in the back, and pin to the earflap. Turn under the raw edge of the fleece opening, and pin to the fleece side of the earflap.

7. With the earflap on your right and the tartan facing you, place the pinned opening under your machine's presser foot. Sew very close to the folded, pinned edge from one side back seam to the other side back seam, maintaining a ⅛˝ to ¼˝ seam allowance.

8. Starting at the center back, topstitch around the circumference of the crown, ½˝ from the pressed edge, pinning if necessary, to secure the lining to the inside of the hat.

9. Hand sew the button securely in place on top of the hat. Insert the needle at the intersection of the fleece lining where the crown sections meet. From there sew through to the outside of the hat where the tartan crown sections meet. Knot on the underside, and trim any stray threads.

the classic sun hat

HAT SIZE: *Women's medium (head circumference 22˝–22½˝)*

We couldn't possibly have a book on hats without including a floppy, casual sun hat. This stylish design is even reversible. The broad brim measures out to 21˝ so that it looks as glamorous as it is practical. Whether you are at the pool, at the beach, or out and about antiquing—wherever the sun is shining—this hat has you covered.

Materials and Supplies

Fabric A: ¾ yard

Fabric B: ¾ yard

Heavyweight fusible interfacing: ⅝ yard for brim stiffening

tips

When selecting fabrics for the hat itself, here are a few things to consider:

- *Quilting-weight cottons are just perfect for this hat. Light and breezy, they will help keep you cool and shady. Anything heavier will result in a hat that may be too warm.*

- *I often make this hat with one bold side, using a complementary smaller print in a color taken from the bold print for the other side.*

- *Consider organics or clean, unused (new) vintage cotton, as well as upcycling something (a sheet or curtain, maybe?) with a great print.*

Cutting

Template patterns are on pullout page P2. Enlarge patterns 200%.

FABRIC A:

Cut 1 brim.

Cut 6 crowns.

FABRIC B:

Cut 1 brim.

Cut 6 crowns.

FUSIBLE INTERFACING:

Cut 1 brim.

ARTIST: Dory Smith Graham, worthygoods
WEBSITE: worthygoods.etsy.com
(handmade accessories)
worthygoodstextile.etsy.com
(organic textiles)
*For more about Dory, see her artist's bio
(page 59).*

CONSTRUCTION

Note: Use a ½˝ seam allowance unless otherwise noted. For all the steps, secure the seams with backstitching at the start and finish.

Brim

1. Fuse the interfacing brim to the wrong side of the Fabric A brim.

2. Fold the Fabric A and Fabric B brim pieces in half, right sides together, as indicated on the pattern. Pin and sew along the straight (center back) edge of each. Press the seams open.

3. Layer the first brim over the other, right sides together. Match up the seams. Pin carefully around the outside edge. Sew around the pinned edge.

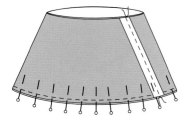

4. Turn the brim right side out, and press the seam flat with an iron on the cotton/steam setting. Press around the entire brim, with the Fabric B side up, making sure to keep both fabrics flat. Take the time to straighten, smooth, and steam; this will make topstitching a breeze.

5. When both sides are neatly pressed, topstitch around the outside edge of the brim starting at the back seam, with the Fabric B side facing up. After the first "lap" around the outside of the brim, continue topstitching—using the latest seam to maintain the seam allowance, sew around and gradually up the entire brim.

Crown

1. Align 3 pairs of Fabric A crown pieces and pin them, right sides together. Sew a side of each pair from the bottom to the dot at the top of the pattern, backstitching at the end of each seam.

2. Open out 2 sewn pairs, align one over the other with right sides together, match the edges at the top, and stitch them together along one edge.

3. Repeat Step 2 with the third crown section. Now all the sections have been joined.

4. To complete the crown, align the outer edges with right sides together, matching the edges at the top, and stitch the final seam.

5. Trim ⅓˝ off the seam allowances from the top of each crown seam. Press the seams flat.

6. Repeat Steps 1–5 with the 6 crown pieces in Fabric B. Press the raw edge of the B crown under ½˝ all the way around.

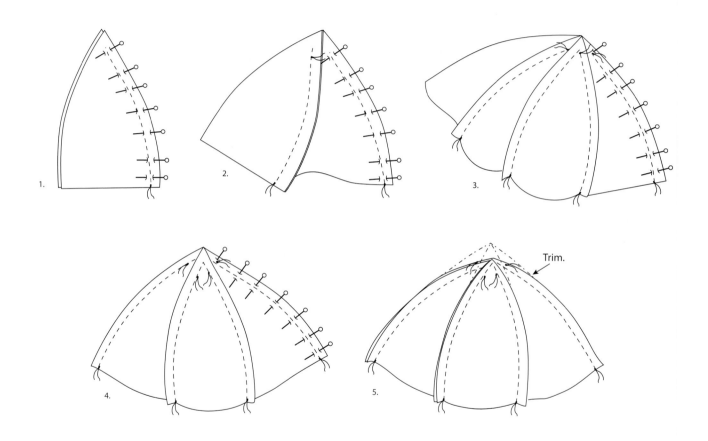

1.

2.

3.

4.

5.

Trim.

Assembly

1. With the raw edge of the brim up and Fabric A on the inside, fold the brim in half gently along the back seam to determine the center front of the brim; mark with a pin. Turn the Fabric A crown right side out and upside down, fitting it just inside the raw edge of the brim. Match a crown seam to the center back seam of the brim; pin. Match the opposite crown seam to the center front of the brim; pin. Evenly space and pin the 4 remaining crown seams along the raw edge of the brim. Sew around the pinned edge using a ½˝ seam allowance.

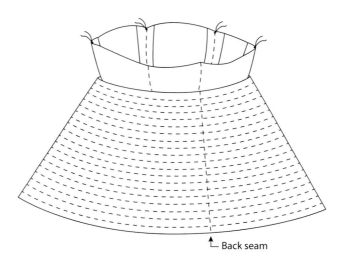

Back seam

2. Press the brim-to-crown seam flat, toward the crown. With Fabric B facing up, push the wrong side of the Fabric A crown up through the brim. Place the Fabric B crown over the Fabric A crown, wrong sides together. Align the seams and pin the pressed edge of the Fabric B crown ¼˝ below the brim-to-crown-A seam. Starting at the back, topstitch around the crown, ⅛˝ from the pressed edge. Clip any stray threads.

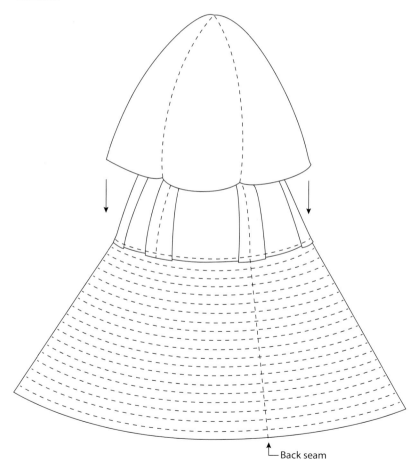

Back seam

whimsical headband

SIZE: *Fits all*

No sewing machine required! Just five simple shapes combine to make this handcrafted headband. Experiment with a variety of materials and shapes to create a truly custom look. The slim design is easy to wear without getting in the way, and with just a few hand stitches for the beads, it adds a simple splash of color suitable for everyday wear or special occasions. This is a perfect project for beginners.

Tammy Gregg was raised by a mother who, when asked, "Can I have this?" would say, "We can make that." Tammy loves to create, she hopes to inspire, and she aches to learn new techniques as well as experiment with new ideas. She began with jewelry, taught herself to sew, created her own patterns, and is now obsessed with creating fun and whimsical hair accessories. Tammy finds it gratifying to take a simple item, such as felt, and produce unusual and playful things for others to enjoy and be inspired by. She sells her wares in local shops and even some not-so-local shops and boutiques. All of her designs are handcrafted with great care and attention to detail. She says she hopes to add a bit of whimsy to your day!

ARTIST: Tammy Gregg
WEBSITE: etsy.com/people/
TopoftheMorning

Materials and Supplies

Stiffened felt in a color of your choice: 1 piece 3˝ × 5˝

Felt in 2 different colors of your choice: 1 piece 4˝ × 5˝ of each color

1˝-wide (or wider) ribbon: 1 piece 6˝ long and 1 piece 10˝ long

¼˝-wide trim: 1 piece 16½˝ long

¼˝-wide metal hair band

Decorative beads and pearls for embellishment

Hot glue gun and glue

Cutting

Template patterns are on page 77.

STIFFENED FELT:

Cut 1 piece 1.

OTHER FELT:

Cut 1 each of pieces 2–5 (whichever felt color you wish).

CONSTRUCTION

Note: Use a ¼˝ seam allowance unless otherwise noted.

1. To cover the metal hair band with the 16½˝-long piece of trim, first fold a raw end of the trim under and glue it ½˝ from an end of the inside of the hair band. Slowly attach the trim with hot glue down to the end, around the end, and up the outside of the hair band. Press down on the trim as you glue so that the glue sets securely. When you reach the opposite end, fold the trim around to the inside again, and fold the raw end under as you did at the beginning.

2. Using the 6˝ piece of ribbon, create a ruffle. Begin by folding back and gluing the raw edge of the ribbon to itself. Glue the front of the ribbon to the back of piece 2, close to the edge of the felt. Gently fold or pleat the ribbon along the back of piece 2, gluing with hot glue as you go. Add extra glue where there are gaps or loose places to secure the ruffle in place. The ruffle will be approximately 2¼˝ long when finished. Use the photo of the finished piece as a guide for ruffle placement.

3. Using hot glue, attach piece 2 with the ruffle to the top of piece 1, being careful to place it where you would like it.

4. Using hot glue, attach piece 3 on top of piece 2, being careful to place it where you would like it.

5. Using a needle and thread, sew embellishments to piece 4, as desired.

6. Using hot glue, attach piece 4 on top of piece 3, being careful to place it where you would like it.

7. Repeat the technique in Step 2 to glue the 10˝ piece of ribbon to piece 1. The ruffle will be approximately 3½˝ long. Use the photo of the finished piece as a guide for ruffle placement.

8. Using hot glue and starting about 1¼˝ from an end of the hair band, attach the focal point piece gently, allowing the piece to bend with the band.

9. Finish the headband by gluing piece 5 to the back of the focal point piece, for security and for a nice finished look.

tip *This whimsical headband is so much fun because it allows you to express your personality. These steps are meant as a guide, but add your own expression by changing colors, ribbons, embellishments, and even the placement of the ruffles. The key is to have fun with it!*

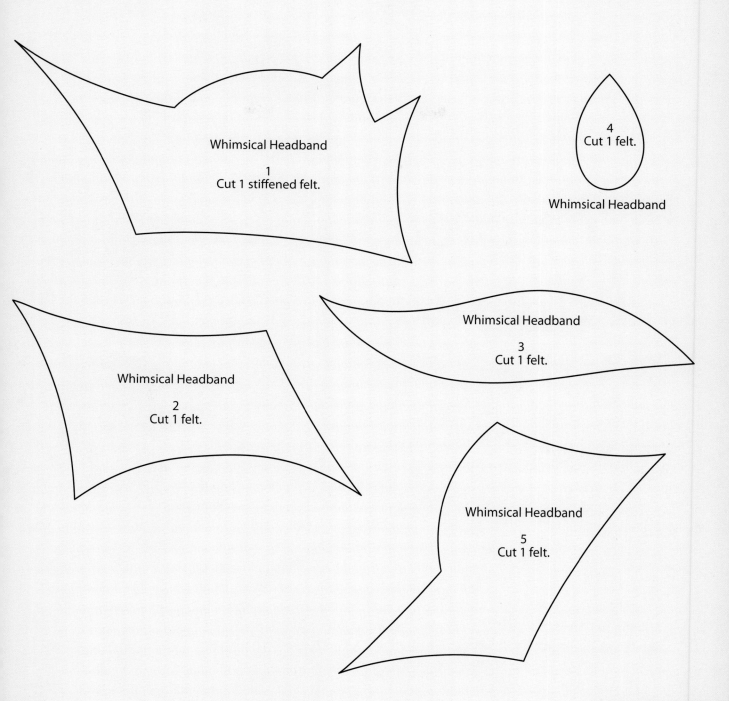

Whimsical Headband

1
Cut 1 stiffened felt.

4
Cut 1 felt.

Whimsical Headband

Whimsical Headband

2
Cut 1 felt.

Whimsical Headband

3
Cut 1 felt.

Whimsical Headband

5
Cut 1 felt.

the chicken little hat

This aviator style hat won't protect your little ones if the sky is falling, but it will keep them cozy and warm when the snow is falling. It is, simply, just adorable. Constructed entirely from fleece, this is a snuggly design that will keep out the cold and wind. Because this hat is perfect for gifting, we have included instructions for three sizes from 6 months to 6 years.

Jen Hagedorn began her crafty endeavors online with hand-dyed clothing and play silks, but the sewing bug won out and she traded her dyes and blanks for sewing machines and fabrics. She retained the Tie Dye Diva name for her line of sewing patterns launched in 2007. Her catalog currently boasts more than 30 downloadable sewing patterns for fleece, quilting cottons, and knit fabrics, and includes patterns for babies, children, adults, and the home. She loves to create wearable designs with a touch of whimsy, like ruffle-bottomed baby wear and this fun chicken hat.

ARTIST: Jen Hagedorn
Tie Dye Diva Patterns
WEBSITES: tiedyediva.etsy.com
tiedyedivadesigns.blogspot.com
facebook.com/tiedyedivapatterns

SIZE CHART

Age	Fits head circumference	Finished unstretched hat circumference
6–12 months	To 18¼˝	17¼˝
1–2 years	To 20˝	19˝
3–6 years	To 21˝	20˝

Materials and Supplies

White polyester fleece (58˝–60˝ wide): ⅓ yard for hat crown and hat band

Yellow or orange polyester fleece: 4˝ × 6˝ scrap for beak

Red polyester fleece: 6˝ × 7˝ scrap for comb

Double-stick fusible web, 12˝ wide (such as Steam-A-Seam 2): 1⅔ yards

½˝-wide hook and loop tape: 1˝ length

Cutting

Template patterns are on pullout page P1. Enlarge patterns 200%. Be sure to cut the crown and band pieces so that the arrows on the pattern are going in the stretchiest direction of the fleece.

WHITE FLEECE:

Cut 4 crowns.
Cut 2 hatbands.

YELLOW OR ORANGE FLEECE:

Cut 2 beaks.

RED FLEECE:

Cut 2 combs.

tip

To cut the curvy pieces accurately and easily, trace the templates for the comb and beak onto double-stick fusible web. Cut around the piece roughly; then peel off one side and stick (don't heat fuse!) the web and remaining paper backing to the fleece. Now cut around the pattern piece neatly, right through both the paper and the fleece. Remove the paper and webbing when you are finished.

CONSTRUCTION

Note: Use a ¼˝ seam allowance.

Fleece does not fray, so seam finishing is not needed. A stretch stitch or narrow zigzag stitch is recommended when sewing parts of the hat that will be stretched when worn, such as the crown seams and crown-to-band seam. If you do not have or do not want to use the stretch stitch, use a longer-length straight stitch; 100% polyester thread also helps with enabling the seams to stretch.

tip

1. Mark the center front of each hat band (where it was folded for cutting) using a pin, washable marker, or chalk.

2. Pin the 2 band pieces with right sides together. Sew all along the underside of the band, including around both chin straps.

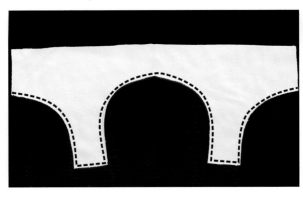

3. Leaving the band wrong side out, open the band up so the side edges are straight.

4. Fold the band in half along the center front marks so that the short side edges are aligned and the right sides of the band are still together. Sew along the short edge.

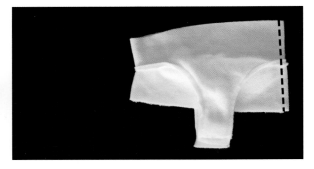

5. Clip the corners and curves, and turn the band right side out using a pointed object such as a chopstick to poke the chin strap corners out square. Lay it so the back seam and center front mark are aligned. Mark the side points with pins, washable marker, or chalk.

6. Pin the beak pieces right sides together; sew, leaving the bottom edge open. Repeat for the comb. Clip the corners and curves. Turn the beak and comb right side out; set aside.

7. Place 2 crown pieces right sides together; insert a pin in the top center of each crown piece, and then finish pinning together. Sew along an edge from the top center to the bottom. Repeat with the remaining 2 crown pieces so that you have 2 crown halves.

8. Lay a crown half right side up. Align the middle of the comb with the center seam, with raw edges aligned. Secure it in place with a pin. Curve and pin the comb piece along the curved edge of the hat. Machine baste the comb in place, sewing close to the edge of the fabric, within the ¼˝ seam allowance.

9. Lay the other half of the hat crown on top so that the hat halves are right sides together and the comb is sandwiched between. Pin and sew the seam.

10. Turn the crown right side out. Center the beak on the front seam, with raw edges aligned, and machine baste in place.

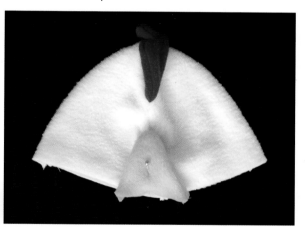

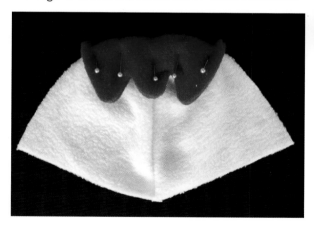

11. Place the band around the crown with right sides together and raw edges aligned. Match the back seams first; then match the front seam of the crown with the center front mark of the band. Match the side seams of the crown with the pins marking the side points of the band. The beak will be tucked between the crown and band. Pin all around, and sew this seam, joining the crown and the band.

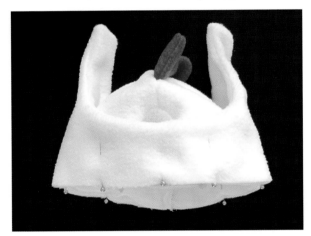

12. Flip the band down, and trim the seam allowances if needed. Center the soft side of the hook and loop tape on the inner side of a chin strap, about ½" away from the bottom edge of the strap. Center the rough piece on the outer side of the other chin strap ½" away from the bottom edge. Sew all around both pieces of hook and loop tape.

double bow headband

Here's an easy, no-sew project with big results—the perfect combination of sassy and sweet. Play with the color of the felt or the size of the strips, or add embellishments, to create a custom look. Quick to make, these make wonderful gifts, great projects for a sleepover, or unique one-time wearables for a special occasion.

Taylor Hart attended art school in Columbus, Ohio, and graduated with a Bachelor's of Fine Arts in still-based media studies in 2003. In 2008 she moved with her husband to Austin, Texas, where she began crocheting and felting as a hobby. That hobby soon grew into a side business selling her pieces in a small boutique. She later started making her own headband patterns and selling them on Etsy. Taylor continues to create unique designs for her Etsy site, Nothing but a Pigeon.

ARTIST: Taylor Hart
WEBSITES: etsy.com/shop/
nothingbutapigeon
nothingbutapigeon.blogspot.com

Materials and Supplies

Felt: 2 sheet 9˝ × 12˝ in complementary colors (project shown uses black and gray)

Black metal headband from arts and crafts store

Glue gun and glue

Cutting

The measurements don't have to be exact for this pattern. Feel free to experiment.

GRAY FELT:

Cut 1 strip 2˝ × 12½˝ for the bow.

Cut 1 strip 2˝ × 4½˝ for the bow.

BLACK FELT:

Cut 1 strip 2˝ × 9˝ for the bow.

Cut 1 strip 1¼˝ × 5˝ for the bow.

Cut 1 strip 2˝ × 5˝ for the backing.

CONSTRUCTION

1. Loop the longer gray strip so that the ends touch each other. With the hot glue gun, glue the 2 loose ends together and onto the opposite side of the strip.

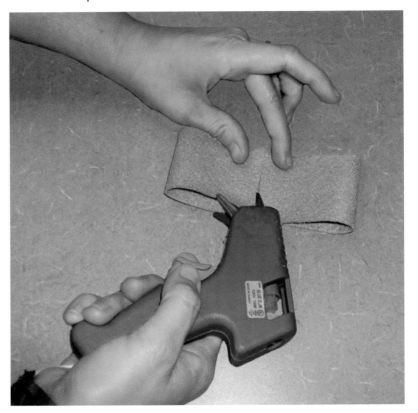

2. Repeat Step 1 with the longest black strip. Place this black bow on top of the gray bow, and glue only in the middle. Leave the bow loose and floppy.

3. Position the bow on the headband, and tack it in place with glue.

4. Loop the remaining gray strip horizontally around the center of the 2 bows that you just placed. Glue tightly around the 2 bows and the headband. The gray strip should be glued all the way until the cut ends are touching each other. Don't worry if the ends overlap.

5. Center the smallest black strip on the previous gray strip, and glue it around the gray strip.

6. Glue the backing black strip underneath the finished bow, concealing the loops that were wrapped around the 2 bows. This step also secures the bows to the headband, making it wearable. Use a lot of hot glue for this part, going almost all the way to the edges of the black strip.

rosey's reversible headscarf

SIZE: *Fits all*

What could be simpler? This pretty little headscarf has rick-rack trim and a sweet button detail to give the back of the scarf some weight … and it is reversible! Embellish and adjust the size as you wish, to create a custom look and fit. If you have a young lady in your life, this is a wonderfully straight-forward project to do with her as an introduction to sewing.

Materials and Supplies

2 pieces of fabric: ⅜ yard each

½˝-wide single-fold bias tape (or you can make your own): 2 yards

Vintage buttons, trims (such as rickrack), or crochet flowers (optional)

Cutting

Template pattern is on pullout page P2. Enlarge pattern 200%.

Cut 1 scarf piece from each fabric.

Carrie Malfeo's life as a designer and mother hen of two amazing nature-loving girls is about all things creative, functional, vintage, and sustainable. These two twigs (girls) inspire her every day to create something unique, inspiring, and as one of a kind as they are. She believes Two Twigs is a result of all the things she holds dear, such as homegrown quality and attention to detail in each piece.

ARTIST: Carrie Malfeo
Two Twigs
WEBSITE: etsy.com/shop/twotwigs22

CONSTRUCTION

Note: Use a ¼˝ seam allowance.

1. Pin the 2 scarf pieces with wrong sides together, and machine baste around all the edges.

2. Sew bias tape to the sides (A and B) of the headscarf using basting stitches. Be sure to pivot cleanly at the point. Trim the raw ends of the tape, if necessary. Fold over the bias tape, and topstitch in place.

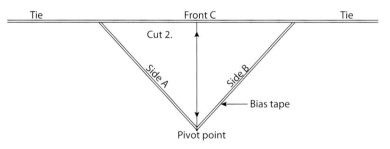

3. Sew bias tape to the front edge (C) as in Step 2, leaving a 10˝ overhang on both sides for ties.

4. Attach trim to the sides, if desired.

5. Hand sew a button or buttons to the point of the headscarf on one or both sides. (This helps hold it in place on windy days.) Knot the ties at the ends to finish.

6. Press, and wear proudly.

the galaxy fascinator

HAT SIZE: *Fits all*

Chic and sophisticated. This is a show-stopping creation that will definitely have all eyes on you. Select complementary tints of tulle and a sweet decorative flower, or get creative and substitute with ornaments of your own. If you can't find the 4-inch straw base for this hat, flip to page 10 for instructions on how to make a fascinator base from scratch.

Eleonora Marchi was born in Florence, Italy. Even as a child, she loved to create things such as dresses and jewelry. At school she studied to become a costume designer, which was a perfect fit, combining all the things she's always loved. After graduating from university, Eleonora worked at The Costume Gallery at Palazzo Pitti in Florence on an old millinery archive. This job gave her the inspiration to start making hair accessories. She's always looking for new materials and techniques. Eleonora even learned the art of making silk flowers with vintage tools that she found in an old laboratory.

ARTIST: Eleonora Marchi
WEBSITE: onyourhead.etsy.com
onyourheads.blogspot.com
facebook.com/pages/On-Your-Head/90209385540

Materials and Supplies

1 blue round straw base, 4˝ in diameter

1 piece of brown (or a color to match your hair) millinery elastic 12˝ long

Tulle, 54˝ wide, in tints from blue to white: ¾ yard total (pieces should be 10˝ × 10˝ minimum)

1 blue rose, 4˝ wide

Styrofoam wig stand

Cutting

From the various colors of tulle, cut 16 squares 10˝ × 10˝ each.

CONSTRUCTION

Note: Use a ¼" seam allowance unless otherwise noted.

1. Stack the tulle squares, fold them in quarters, and pin them together. Cut the folded fabrics into a quarter-circle. Open the cut fabrics, and stitch the circles together at the middle point with nylon thread.

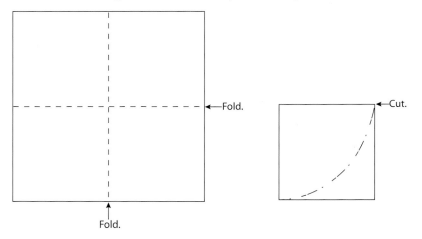

2. Make 2 small holes in opposite edges of the straw base. Knot the elastic at an end and thread the other end through a hole from the top to the underside and back up through the other hole from the underside to the top. Knot the elastic at the unknotted end, and trim any excess elastic from the knots. (The strap will be loose in the middle.)

3. Stitch the middle point of the 16 pieces of tulle to the middle of the straw base.

4. Put the hat on the wig stand and hold it with a pin.

5. Loosely fold the 16 pieces of tulle from point A to the middle and secure them in place with a pin.

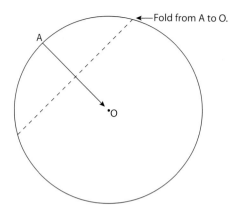

Fold from A to O.

6. Fold from point B to point C, and secure with a pin. This fold creates the shape of the back side of the hat.

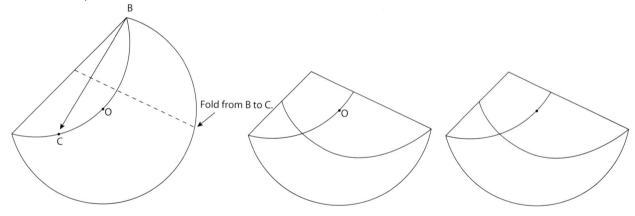

Fold from B to C.

7. Stitch the pinned points down with nylon thread.

8. Take all the single layers on the right part of the hat and fold them so that they stand up perpendicular to the middle of the hat, holding them with pins until you create a shape you like. Stitch in place with nylon thread.

9. Stitch the blue rose to the middle of the hat, covering the previously stitched point.

monster cap

HAT SIZE: *Head circumference up to 21˝*

Monsters, monsters, everywhere! Whether they pull it over their faces and pretend to be monsters, or leave it where it is meant to be on top of their heads, this hat will get a lot of use from the youngsters in your life. And it keeps them nice and toasty. Constructed using a combination of nice stretchy knits, this hat is wonderfully modern, but still has great kid appeal. Have fun switching up the appliqué embellishments.

An architectural drafter by trade, *Andrea Roman* is a self-taught crafter and textile designer with a focus on modern boy and gender-neutral children's patterns. In 2009, she created T♥toz Designs, named after her father, to commemorate his life and the blessings he gave, and as a reminder to keep a balance of creativity in her own life. Recently she became a designer for Go Mama Go Designs, LLC, makers of safer alternatives for crib bedding. She resides in the Midwest with her supportive husband and a young son, who gives her an infinite amount of design inspiration.

ARTIST: Andrea Z. Roman

T♥toz Designs

WEBSITES: spoonflower.com/profiles/ttoz

ttoz.etsy.com

Materials and Supplies

Knit fabric: ½ yard for hat exterior (face)

Knit fabric: ½ yard for lining

Fabric scraps for appliqués (all sizes are minimums):

6˝ × 6˝ white (eye)

2˝ × 2˝ black (pupil)

1¼˝ × 6˝ color of your choice (nose)

2˝ × 5˝ color of your choice (teeth)

5˝ × 9½˝ color of your choice (horns)

Paper-backed double-sided fusible web, 20˝ wide, for the face: approximately ¼ yard

Cutting

Template patterns are on pullout page P2. Enlarge patterns 200%. When cutting the hat exterior (face) fabric, fold it right sides together with the stretch going perpendicular to the fold line.

MAIN FACE FABRIC:

Cut 1 Monster Cap.

LINING FABRIC:

Cut 1 Monster Cap.

APPLIQUÉS:

Follow the manufacturer's instructions to iron the fusible web to the appliqué fabrics. (See Fusible Appliqué Instructions, page 97, for additional information.)

Cut 2 teeth.

Cut 2 side eyes.

Cut 1 center eye.

Cut 3 pupils for the eyes.

Cut 2 horns.

Nose fabric is already cut to size.

CONSTRUCTION

Note: Use a ⅜˝ seam allowance.

1. With the main fabric hat folded with right sides together as it was cut out, pin the back seam together and stitch. Flip the hat right side out.

2. Repeat Step 1 with the lining fabric, only do not turn it right side out.

3. Adhere the appliqué features to the right side of the main fabric using the photo (page 94) of the finished hat as your guide, or by all means, use your own and your kid's creativity! The fusible web is the only thing necessary to keep everything in place, but for added security and finishing, you can topstitch along the edges with matching or contrasting thread.

> ### Note:
> *Align the raw edge at the top of the horn with the raw edge at the top of the hat. Match the notch on each horn to the notch on the top of the hat.*

4. Place the lining fabric over the main fabric and smooth to fit, matching the notches and back seams (the right side of the lining should face the right side—the appliquéd face—of the main fabric). Pin together the bottom edge, and sew all the way around the bottom seamline.

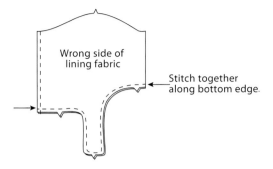

Wrong side of lining fabric

Stitch together along bottom edge.

5. Trim down the seam allowance at the curves if needed (being sure not to cut the stitching) and turn right side out. Press around the bottom edge, and topstitch around the perimeter of the bottom edge with matching or contrasting thread.

6. With the lining facing out and the main fabric facing in, fold the hat through the center of the horns and straps so the back seam lines up with the center of the front. Stitch through all 4 layers along the top edge and zigzag stitch or serge the seam allowance to reinforce. Flip right side out, and you are ready to roar!

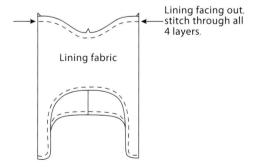

Lining facing out, stitch through all 4 layers.

Lining fabric

Fusible Appliqué Instructions

1. *Trace all the parts of the appliqué design onto the paper side of the fusible web. Trace each layer of the design separately. Label each piece for easy placement.*

2. *Rough cut around the appliqué shapes leaving a small margin around each.*

3. *Iron each fusible web shape to the wrong side of the appropriate fabric. Cut on the tracing lines, and peel the paper backing off the fusible web. A thin layer of fusible web will remain on the wrong side of the fabric—this will adhere the appliqué pieces to the main fabric.*

4. *Position the pieces on the main fabric. Press to fuse in place.*

5. *Optional: Machine stitch around the appliqué pieces using a zigzag, satin, or blanket stitch. Stitch any other lines to add detail as desired.*

old-school cap

HAT SIZE: *Fits all adults*

Struggling with what to make for the men and boys in your life? This classic cap might be the answer. Gender-neutral in its design, thanks to the adjustable closures, this hat is crying out to be customized. Select a timeless canvas, a handsome tweed, or even a novelty print. Add embellishments, signatures, photo transfers, or fabric paint to make a bespoke hat.

Gailen Runge started quilting as a hobby in 1991. For a short time (in between publishing jobs), she operated a custom quiltmaking business. She found a happy home as creative director at C&T Publishing (and its imprint Stash Books) and continues to sew in her spare time. With the arrival of her two children, quilting gave way to smaller, less time- and space-consuming projects such as garments, purses and other accessories, and miscellaneous stuffed animal accoutrements. Gailen is looking forward to her children's eventual independence so she can spend more time in the studio. She loves to try sewing new things and is always excited to figure out how to make them work.

ARTIST: Gailen Runge

Materials

Wool, twill, denim, or other fun fabric: ⅓ yard for cap

Cotton in complementary color: ½ yard for lining (fat quarter would work)

½˝-wide double-fold bias tape: 1 pack (3 yards)

Timtex interfacing: 2 rectangles 6˝ × 8˝ for bill

Stiff fusible interfacing, 20˝ wide (such as Pellon Craft Fuse): ⅜ yard

Lighter-weight fusible interfacing, 20˝ wide: ⅛ yard

Vest buckle

Self-cover button (optional)

Cutting

Template patterns are on pullout page P2. Enlarge patterns 200%.

Note:

Before cutting the 2 cap fronts and 1 bill piece from the cap fabric, fuse the stiff interfacing onto the back of the fabric. Make sure to mark the eyelet placement on the cap pieces (if you're going to add eyelets).

CAP FABRIC:

Cut 2 fronts (1 and 1 reversed).

Cut 2 sides (1 and 1 reversed).

Cut 2 backs (1 and 1 reversed).

Cut 2 bills.

Cut 1 rectangle 2˝ × 5˝ for the adjustable back strap.

Cut 1 rectangle 2˝ × 4˝ for the buckle side of the back strap.

COTTON LINING:

Cut 1 bias rectangle 2˝ × 25˝ for the facing.

LIGHTWEIGHT INTERFACING:

Cut 2 rectangles 2˝ × 12˝ for the facing.

BIAS TAPE:

Cut 3 strips each 15˝ long.

Cut 1 strip 8˝ long to face the back opening.

TIMTEX:

Cut 2 bills.

CONSTRUCTION

Use a ⅜″ seam allowance unless otherwise noted.

Back straps

1. Fold the 2″ × 5″ cap fabric rectangle in half, with right sides together and long edges aligned. Sew along the aligned long edge with a ¼″ seam allowance.

2. Turn the tube right side out, center the seam, and press the seam open.

3. Tuck an end inside the tube ¼″.

4. Topstitch around 3 sides of the tube approximately ⅛″ from the edges, sealing the tucked-in end and leaving the opposite end open. Set aside.

5. Repeat Steps 1 and 2 with the 2″ × 4″ strip, leaving both short ends open. Topstitch the 2 longer edges. Set aside.

Facing

1. Fuse the lightweight interfacing to the back of the cotton facing strip.

2. Fold the top edge of the cotton facing strip over lengthwise (wrong sides together) ½″. Topstitch this folded edge ⅛″ from the fold. With the folded edge at the top and the interfacing side down, fold in the short right-hand end (wrong sides together) ¼″ and topstitch. Set aside.

3. To prepare a facing for the back opening, open up the 8″ strip of double-fold bias tape, and trim ¾″ off along the length (this is 1½ of the folded sections, leaving 2 folded sections and a ¼″ seam allowance).

4. Press the ¼″ seam allowance part flat (flattening that fold).

Eyelets

Eyelets are a traditional detail on baseball caps, but you can choose to ignore them. Your machine might have an eyelet stitch. If it does, use it! If it doesn't, you can use a zigzag stitch and a little practice.

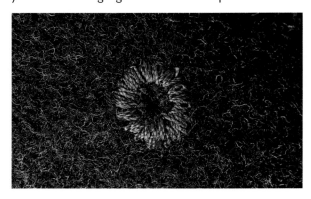

1. Set your machine for a zigzag stitch that is medium width (2.5 on some machines) and very close together but not quite a satin stitch (0.4 on some machines). The width is the width of the visible stitches, not the size of the center hole. The size of the center eyelet hole is controlled by the distance of the stitches from each other and the amount you rotate with each step. The closer the stitches or the smaller the rotation, the tighter the

eyelet circle. Use the needle-down position if you have it.

2. Insert the needle next to the eyelet mark, and take a zigzag stitch out and back.

3. Lift the presser foot and rotate the fabric around the needle a little bit (about 1/16 of the circle). Take another stitch.

4. Repeat Step 3 until you pivot around the circle once. Continue around the circle once or twice more, aiming the stitches for any gaps in your first go-round.

5. For the last stitch, change the distance to 0 and take a stitch in place. Cut the threads.

6. Use an awl or one side of small, sharp scissors to poke the fabric out of the eyelet's center hole. If the eyelet is large enough, use the scissors to cut out the center; just don't cut the stitches.

Crown

1. Pin the 2 front crown pieces right sides together, and stitch the center seam. Press the seam open.

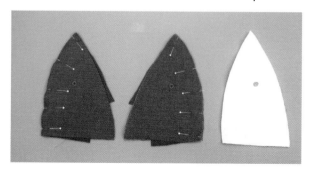

2. Repeat Step 1 with the remaining pieces, pairing the side with the back and the reverse side with the reverse back.

3. Place 2 of the pairs together, pinning and sewing the front to a side/back pair, starting 3/8˝ from the edge at the top of the hat.

4. Repeat Step 4 with the remaining side/back pair.

5. Sew up the back seam. Press the seam allowances open.

6. On the wrong side of the crown, pin a 15˝-long strip of bias tape over the center-front-to-the-center-back seam, centering it on the seamline.

Note:

If you're using 1/2˝ bias tape, trim the seam allowances to approximately 1/8˝–3/16˝. When you topstitch the bias on, be sure to catch the seam allowances under the bias.

7. Topstitch close to both edges. Trim any excess bias tape off at the ends.

8. Repeat Steps 6 and 7 with the remaining 2 pieces of bias tape.

9. Pin the bias tape for the back facing to the back opening, with right sides together, aligning the single-layer edge of the bias with the raw edge of the opening.

10. Sew around the back opening with a ¼˝ seam allowance. Turn the bias tape to the inside of the hat and press.

11. Topstitch close to the edge of the bias tape.

Bill

1. Pin the bill pieces right sides together. Sew around the outside curved part of the bill. Turn right side out and press flat.

2. Slide the 2 layers of Timtex into the bill. Push, pull, slide, and tug the curved part of the Timtex into the curved part of the bill, making the seamline as smooth as possible. Pin the bill in place along the inside edge.

3. Topstitch around the curve ¼˝ from the edge. Repeat twice more, ¼˝ apart, for 3 rows of stitching. To sew around this curve smoothly, put the brim under the needle at the desired position. Plant your right pointer finger on your sewing machine even with the needle and against the edge of the bill. Stitch around the bill, using your left hand to keep the hat pushed gently but firmly against your finger.

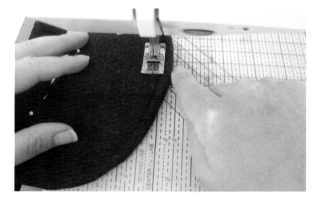

4. Baste the inside curve closed, ⅛″ from the edge.

(The 2 pointy corners of the bill will get a little rough and not quite even during this process. That's fine. Any defects here will be hidden behind the facing.)

Assembly

1. Feed the buckle onto the short back strap. Fold the back strap in half widthwise.

2. Position the strap on one side of the back opening, ½″ from the bottom of the hat, with the raw edges ½″ in from the hat edge. Topstitch it in place along the top-stitching line that holds the back facing down.

3. Position the second back strap on the other side of the back opening and repeat Step 2.

4. Align the center of the bill with the center front seam of the hat and pin the bill in place, matching the raw edges, to the right side of the hat. Stitch the

2 pieces together with a ¼″ seam allowance. It will feed through the machine more easily if the bill is the bottom piece.

5. Starting with the folded end of the cotton facing against the back opening, pin the cap to the facing, with raw edges aligned and right sides together. The bill will be sandwiched between the facing and the cap. Pin from the inside of the cap, making sure the facing will be on the bottom under the presser foot.

6. Stitch a ⅜″ seam allowance around the bottom of the hat, stopping 2″ from the end.

7. Measure how much facing you need, add ¼″ to the measurement, and trim the facing. Turn under the end ¼″ and topstitch.

8. Continue sewing on the facing. Press the facing to the inside of the hat.

9. Pin the facing smooth if necessary and topstitch the bottom of the hat ¼″ from the edge.

10. Press the hat and shape the bill as desired.

11. If desired, cover a button with matching fabric and sew it to the exterior top center of the cap.

retro flat cap

HAT SIZE: *Head circumference 22½" to 23"*

Worn by celebrities around the globe, the classic flat cap is coming back into fashion with a bang. By using the great instructions that follow, this hat is a lot easier to make than it looks.

This pattern is sized just for the men, so find some great retro fabrics and create a custom hat to keep or gift.

Bonnie Shaffer is a milliner who makes retro-style hats for men and women. The fabulous quality of vintage fabrics really inspires her. She has a huge collection of vintage wools and buckles and is always on the hunt for more. Bonnie has worked as a costume properties artisan, making accessories for the stage for more than ten years. She has collaborated with a variety of designers from around the world and has created everything from foul-mouthed puppets to leather gorgets to spats, crowns, and sword belts. She enjoys it all but absolutely loves making hats and hopes you enjoy them, too!

ARTIST: Bonnie Shaffer
WEBSITE: etsy.com/shop/bonniesknitting

Materials and Supplies

Wool: ⅝ yard

Visor board or Timtex: 1 piece 6˜ × 8½˜

Fusible interfacing (I used 860F from Pellon): ¾ yard

Cotton fabric: ⅝ yard for lining

Double-stick tape

Clothespins

Cutting

Template patterns are on pullout page P1. Enlarge patterns 200%.

Note:

Except when cutting the visor board insert pattern, lay the 3 pattern pieces on the straight of grain. Be sure to mark the center fronts in the seam allowances of the fabric for the top and sideband pieces. When cutting the wool, be sure to match the plaids in your layout.

WOOL:

Cut 1 top.

Cut 1 sideband.

Cut 2 bills.

COTTON LINING:

Cut 1 top.

Cut 1 sideband.

INTERFACING:

Once you've traced the interfacing shapes, trim away the ⅜˜ seam allowances.

Cut 1 top.

Cut 1 sideband.

Cut 2 bills.

VISOR BOARD OR TIMTEX:

Cut 1 bill insert.

CONSTRUCTION

Note: Use a ⅜˜ seam allowance.

1. Fuse the interfacing to the wool for the top, sideband, and bill pieces (use a pressing cloth).

2. On the wool top, pin and sew the center back dart to the dot. Trim the seam allowance and press open. (Note: The photos show solid canvas rather than wool so the stitching lines are more visible.)

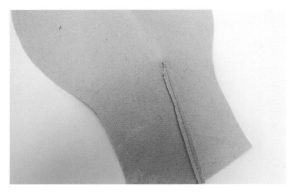

3. Staystitch ¼˝ inside the inner curves of the top between the dots. Clip the curves.

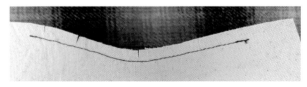

4. Pin the sideband to the top with right sides together, matching the center front marks.

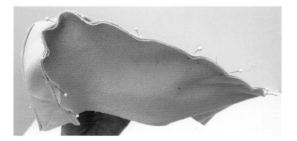

5. Sew the seam. Clip the seam allowance all around, trim the seam allowance to ¼˝, and press open. Turn right side out, and topstitch ⅛˝ on each side of the seam.

6. Pin 2 wool bill pieces right sides together, and stitch the outer seam. Clip the curves, and trim to ¼˝. (Don't lose your center front mark here!)

7. Place double-stick tape at intervals across the outer edge of the visor board to hold the fabric in place.

8. With the bill section wrong side out, line up the center fronts of the visor board and the fabric between the seam allowances. Press to make the tape stick. Use a clothespin on the right side to hold the pieces in place.

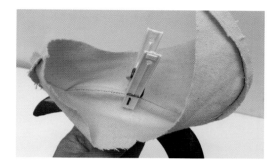

9. Work from the center to the edges in this manner, placing clothespins as you go. Hand baste the outer edge of the bill through the visor board to hold it in place for sewing.

10. Topstitch ⅛˝ from the edge of the bill. Remove the basting.

11. Pin the bill to the right side of the sideband, matching the center front notch and ending at the side notches. Stitch and clip the curves of the seam allowance.

12. Repeat Steps 2–5 with the lining fabric.

13. Insert the wool hat, right side out, into the lining, right side in. Pin the lining to the wool, matching the center back dart and seams. Pin to just inside each edge of the bill, leaving most of the bill free for turning to the right side.

14. Stitch around the bottom edge of the hat, leaving an opening at the bill. Clip the seam allowance. Grade the seams (trim the layers to different lengths so the seam allowance is not thick and unwieldy).

15. Turn the hat right side out through the opening at the center front.

16. Press from the inside, rolling the lining in ⅛˝ or so. Press from the right side.

17. Slipstitch the remaining lining in place.

18. Try on the cap, and pin the center front of the hat to the bill where you would like it to stay. Invisibly tack the hat to the bill to keep it in place.

betty jane's rain hat

HAT SIZE: *Fits most head sizes (circumference 21˝–22½˝)*

When the weather is too windy for an umbrella, or if it is only a little bit drizzly out, or if you just don't want to carry around a bulky brolly, pull out this little hat and you are all set. This hat is a true vintage throwback, and so practical and pretty. Constructed using vinyl and ribbon, this is a must-have for ladies on the go. Instructions are included for a smart carrying pouch, too.

Jenifer Sult began sewing as a child and was drawn to the magic of taking an ordinary piece of fabric and turning it into something useful and beautiful. Today she works as a professional seamstress and designer. Being able to make a living by sewing is a dream come true—one that is only possible with the support of her family. Jenifer's designs are inspired by her attraction to scraps of fabric and vintage pieces of clothing, which she assembles into something new. She particularly loves to make hats and accessories because their small size showcases the details that make them special. She loves to include hand-worked elements in a piece and thinks that seeing the evidence of the craftsperson behind an object is part of what gives that object depth and sincerity. Jenifer sees accessories as a key element in expressing your personality and style.

ARTIST: Jenifer Sult

J Sult Handmade

WEBSITES: cutandsewn.etsy.com

jenifersult.wordpress.com

Materials and Supplies

Light- to medium-weight clear vinyl, such as Quilter's Vinyl: ½ yard (54˝ wide) *or* 1 yard (18˝ wide) for hat

Fabric remnant: 9˝ × 12˝ for pouch

Ribbon: 1 yard for pouch

3-yard package double-fold narrow (¼˝) bias tape for hat

Small objects to use as pattern weights

Hints for Working with Vinyl

- *Vinyl fabric has no grain, so pattern pieces can be laid out in any direction.*

- *Vinyl will stick to the presser foot on your machine, preventing the fabric from moving forward. To avoid this, you can cover the bottom of the presser foot with transparent adhesive tape, use a Teflon foot or a roller foot, or lay transparent tracing paper over the seam as you sew it. Sew right through the tracing paper, and then gently rip the paper off on the perforated line that your stitches have created. Remove tiny pieces of paper from under the stitches with tweezers.*

- *If the vinyl becomes creased or wrinkled, you can lay it out flat on your ironing surface, place a piece of cotton fabric or a towel over the vinyl, and press using a warm iron and continuous motion.*

- *Pins will leave permanent holes in vinyl, so use pattern weights or small heavy objects to weight your paper templates down instead of pinning them to the material.*

CONSTRUCTION

Note: Use a ¼˝ seam allowance for all the hat seams and a ½˝ seam allowance on the carrying pouch.

Cutting

Template patterns are on pullout page P2. Enlarge patterns 200%. Template patterns include the seam allowances.

VINYL:

Cut 1 top.

Cut 2 sides.

Cut 1 brim.

FABRIC:

Cut 1 rectangle 9˝ × 12˝ for the pouch.

Hat

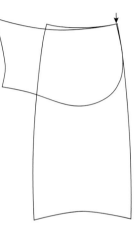

1. Match the front edges of the top and a side together. If you need to pin the pieces together, be sure that the pins are only in the seam allowance so that you do not leave holes in the finished hat. Sew carefully from the front edge to the back edge, adjusting the top piece to fit around the side. Do not worry if the 2 pieces end up slightly uneven at the end of the seam at the back; a small difference in length (about ¼˝) is acceptable and can be trimmed away after both side seams are sewn.

2. Repeat Step 1 with the remaining side. Trim the seam allowance on these 2 seams down to ⅛˝.

3. Cover the seams with bias tape by folding the bias tape over the seam allowance and covering the stitching line completely. Sew through both the tape and the seam, being sure to catch both edges of the tape in your stitching. Slightly stretch the tape as you sew around the curve. Cut the end of the tape even with the front and back edges.

4. Sew bias tape along the back and neck edge from front corner to front corner in the same manner.

5. Fold the brim in half along the dotted line indicated on the pattern. Place the brim inside the hat, with raw edges together, and match the center front notches. Sew from the center front to one end of the

brim, and then repeat for the other side. When the brim is folded out, the seam allowance should be toward the outside of the hat. Trim the seam allowance down to ⅛″ and even with the front edge of the sides.

6. Cut a 45″ piece of bias tape. Fold the tape in half widthwise, and mark this center point with a pin. Fold the brim toward the inside of the hat; match the center of the bias tape with the center front notch. Starting at the center front, sew the bias tape over the brim seam and down one side of the hat. When you reach the end of the vinyl, keep sewing down the length of the remaining bias tape, sewing the tape closed. Repeat for the other side.

7. Flip the brim out, and press the bias tape down flat over the brim with your fingers. Carefully sew the fold of the bias tape down to the brim.

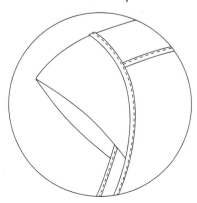

Carrying pouch

1. Clip ½″ into the fabric on both long edges, 2½″ from a short end. (This short end will be the top.) To hem the opening for the casing, fold the fabric that is above the notch on each side over ¼″ twice. Topstitch close to the first fold on the inside.

2. To form the casing, fold over the top ½″ and press in place. Fold again 1″ down so that the first fold is now even with the notches, and topstitch in place close to the fold.

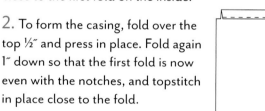

3. Fold the pouch in half lengthwise. Begin sewing at the notch, using a ½″ seam allowance. Sew to the corner, pivot, and sew to the fold, making sure to backstitch at the beginning and end of the seam.

4. To prevent fraying, finish the seam allowance with a zigzag stitch, with pinking shears, or by serging close to the stitch line. Trim the seam allowance, and clip diagonally across the corner.

5. Turn the pouch right side out and press. Feed the ribbon through the casing, and tie the ends together.

singing in the rain hat

Are you tempted by all of the laminated cotton available but just don't know what to make with it? This is the project for you. This hat uses oilcloth or laminated cotton to its best advantage in an all-weather pageboy design. If you can't find a cotton laminate you like, you can always use a laminating product such as HeatnBond Iron-On Vinyl instead. Or interface some quilting-weight cotton or canvas to create a classic version of a pageboy.

From a blog about the journey of a young quilting mom to designing patterns for Moda, CaraQuilts Designs has morphed and changed into a passion for sharing quilting with others. *Cara Wilson* is addicted to fabric and color. Nothing makes her happier than marrying a design with the perfect fabric so that both are better together than apart. CaraQuilts Designs provides patterns and handmade items with a modern spin on classic designs. Making hard and time-consuming things quickly and easily is the goal of most of Cara's patterns, and quality, comfort, and classic designs define her quilted wraps and other handmade goods.

ARTIST: Cara Wilson
CaraQuilts Designs
WEBSITE: caraquilts.com

Materials and Supplies

Quilting cotton fabric: ⅓ yard for lining

Laminate quilting cotton: ½ yard for outside of hat

Fusible batting: ¼ yard (if you don't have fusible batting, use 2 layers of regular batting)

Cutting

Template patterns are on pages 117.

COTTON LINING FABRIC:

Cut 1 top.

Cut 2 strips 3¾˝ × 12½˝.

LAMINATE FABRIC:

Cut 1 top.

Cut 2 brims.

Cut 2 strips 3¾˝ × 12½˝.

Cut 1 strip 3½˝ × 24½˝.

FUSIBLE BATTING:

Cut 1 brim.

CONSTRUCTION

Note: Use a ¼˝ seam allowance unless otherwise noted. See Hints for Working with Vinyl (page 109) when sewing the laminate fabric.

Brim

1. Layer the laminate fabrics right sides together on top of the batting piece. Stitch around the outside curve of the brim using a ¼˝ seam allowance. Use pinking shears to trim the seam allowance, being careful not to cut the stitching. If you don't have pinking shears, use regular scissors and cut every ½˝ to just above the stitching.

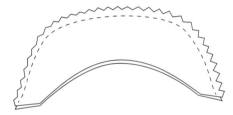

2. Turn the brim right side out. Using your fingers, press the seam of the brim. Topstitch ⅛˝ from the edge all around the outside curve. Stitch another row ¼˝ from the line you just stitched. Stitch a row every ¼˝–½˝ so you have 4–6 rows. On some fabrics these lines of stitching will really show; you can free-motion quilt if you prefer. Set the brim aside for assembly.

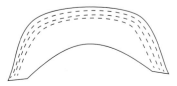

Band

1. Fold the 3½˝ × 24½˝ strip in half crosswise with right sides together. Stitch along the short ends, creating a circle. Finger-press the seam allowance open.

2. Turn right side out and topstitch ⅛˝ on either side of the seam, or use a zigzag stitch and go right over the seam.

3. Fold the entire band wrong side together lengthwise so that the band is now 1¾˝ wide. Topstitch the folded edge. Set aside.

Sides

1. Stitch the 3¾˝ × 12½˝ cotton lining strips right sides together along both of the 3¾˝ ends, creating a circle. Finger-press the seams open.

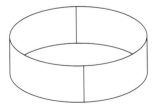

2. Turn right side out and topstitch the seams, either ⅛˝ on either side or with a zigzag down the center.

3. Repeat Steps 1 and 2 with the laminate 3¾˝ × 12½˝ strips.

Bucket

1. Finger-press the cotton lining top circle in half along the edges so you can tell where the halfway point is, and then fold in half again the opposite way and finger-press again.

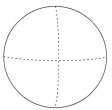

2. Match up the seams of the side lining unit, flatten it out, and press the ends so you can see where the halfway points are.

3. With wrong sides out and right sides together, line up the pressed lines on the cotton lining top circle with the seams and pressed lines on the cotton lining side. Pin at those 4 markings. Midway between pins insert another pin, easing the pieces together. Continue inserting pins until you have about 16 pins.

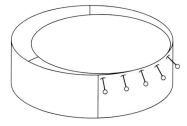

4. Stitch ¼˝ from the edge of the circle all the way around. Remove the pins and use pinking shears to trim around the edge, being careful to not cut the stitch line.

5. Repeat Steps 1–4 with the laminate fabric.

Assembly

1. Turn the laminate bucket right side out and insert it into the lining bucket, which is wrong side out. The right sides of the fabrics should be facing each other. Insert the band, matching the seams, between the laminate and lining buckets, with the folded edge down. Fold the brim in half and finger-press the center of the inside curve. Line it up with the center pressed marks of the buckets. The order from the inside out is laminate bucket (right side out), band, brim (top facing the laminate bucket), and lining bucket. Pin. Rotate a quarter-turn, line up the marks again, and pin. Repeat all the way around the hat.

2. Go back to the brim, ease it up to the bucket and band, and pin as you go. You will need to pin every inch or so. The narrow ends of the brim will stick up past the buckets. They will be cut off once the piece is stitched together.

3. Add pins to the back of the piece, making sure to catch the band as well as both buckets.

4. Stitch ¼˝ from the edge, leaving a 2˝–3˝ opening at the back for turning. Check to make sure you've caught all the layers, especially the brim, before removing the pins. Remove the pins.

5. With pinking shears, trim around the seam as much as you can, being careful not to cut through the stitch lines. The brim may be too thick to easily cut through. Just do the best you can.

6. Reach inside the opening you left and grab the brim, fold it in half, and pull it through the opening, turning the piece right side out. Push the lining into the laminate bucket. Pull the edge as much as you can so that the lining is not showing from the outside.

7. Fold the pieces from the opening into the seam and hand stitch closed. Topstitch ⅛˝ around the bottom of the band, going over the brim.

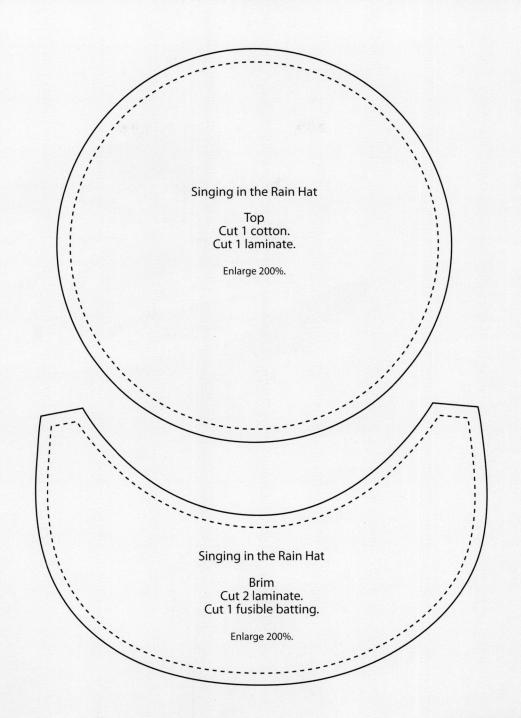

Singing in the Rain Hat

Top
Cut 1 cotton.
Cut 1 laminate.

Enlarge 200%.

Singing in the Rain Hat

Brim
Cut 2 laminate.
Cut 1 fusible batting.

Enlarge 200%.

lady gray

This is a classy thrift twist on the classic bucket hat. This one has a brim that tapers a bit in the back so that you can wear your hair in a ponytail if you like. The fun bit begins with repurposing a women's size medium dress shirt. This shirt already had some great rickrack detailing, so be sure to watch for special embellishments when you look for a thrift shirt of your own. Much of the detailing came from trying to use all the bits and pieces from the shirt with as little waste as possible—so use the detailing from your shirt to inspire creative touches of your own.

Susanne Woods has been sewing since she could thread a needle. She goes to garage sales with her mom every weekend. Buying something new is a last resort. She and her husband raise their two young boys and operate a boutique retail furniture consignment store. She also is working toward her postgraduate degree in interior design.

ARTIST: Susanne Woods

WEBSITES: beyondthekids.com
chameleonconsignment.com

Materials and Supplies

Gray wool/rayon blend felt (20% or 30% wool content is preferable): ¼ yard

Black quilting cotton: ¼ yard

Shape-Flex or similar lightweight fusible interfacing: 1 yard

1 medium long-sleeved button-down shirt with at least 3˝ cuffs (with 2 buttons on each cuff) and single-buttoned collar

1¼˝-wide ribbon in coordinating color: ¾ yard

Cutting

Template patterns are on pullout page P1. Enlarge patterns 200%.

SHAPE-FLEX:

Cut 1 top.

Cut 4 crowns.

Cut 2 brims.

WOOL FELT:

Cut 2 crowns.

BLACK FABRIC:

Cut 1 brim.

SHIRT:

See Deconstructing the Shirt (page 120).

Cut 2 crowns from a sleeve (fold the sleeve in half lengthwise, right sides together, and cut both pieces at once).

Cut 1 top from the other sleeve.

Cut 1 top from the shirtfront (paying careful attention to where you would like to have the line of buttons; the project hat has the row of buttons slightly offset to the right of center).

Cut 1 brim from the back panel.

Deconstructing the Shirt

1. Cut off the cuffs from the sleeves of the shirt as close as possible to the edges of the cuffs, but be careful not to cut into the cuffs themselves.

2. Remove the collar from the top of the shirt in the same manner.

3. Button up the front of the shirt and cut off the sleeves at the shoulder seams.

4. Cut through the length of the sleeves along each seam.

5. Cut through the side seams of the body of the shirt, and cut at the shoulder seams.

This should leave you with 1 front panel (with buttons), 1 back panel, 2 sleeves, 1 collar, and 2 cuffs.

CONSTRUCTION

Note: Use a ½˝ seam allowance unless otherwise noted.

1. Fuse the interfacing to the wrong side of the shirting crown pieces, the felt crown pieces, the shirting top with the buttons, the black brim piece, and the shirting brim piece.

2. Fold the shirting brim piece in half crosswise, right sides facing. Stitch the 2 smaller ends together to form a circle. Press the seam open. Repeat with the black fabric brim piece.

3. Layer the black and shirting brims, right sides facing. Stitch together the 2 brim pieces along the outside edge. Turn and press. Set aside.

4. Layer the wool felt crown pieces, right sides facing. Stitch the 2 crown pieces together at each end to form a circle. Press the seams open. Repeat with the shirting fabric crown pieces.

5. Cut 12 notches ¼˝ deep around the edge of the 2 shirting top pieces (1 notch every 2˝ or so).

6. Pin the top piece that has buttons to the wool felt crown along the top edge, right sides facing. Stitch and press the seams open. Turn right side out. Repeat with the top without buttons and the shirting crown to make the lining.

7. Keeping the lining form inside out, insert it inside the shirting/wool form, wrong sides together. Match the seams, and baste ¼˝ from the raw edge along the base of the crown.

8. Unbutton each of the cuffs. Button the cuffs together so that you have a rectangle approximately 19˝ in length. Pin the cuff onto the outside of the wool crown, aligning the buttoned portion with the side seam you prefer and positioning the top of the cuff approximately 2˝

from the base of the crown. This height may need to be adjusted based on the width of the cuff. Mine were 4˝ cuffs. Stitch into place along the top edge. The cuff length will not go around the full circumference of the hat, but don't worry—that is what the collar is for! Flip up the cuffs to give yourself room to work on the next step.

9. Pin the brim to the crown so that the raw edges are on the inside of the hat, aligning the center back seam on the brim with the center back mark on the crown. Stitch into place. Trim the seam to ¼˝, and press it open inside the hat. A tailor's ham will make the seams easier to press, or you can use a rolled-up towel. The most important part of this step is to get a good fit on the inside, which means you need as flat a seam as possible.

10. Flip the cuff piece back down over the crown/brim seam. Unbutton the lower button of the cuff to release the tension and adjust the cuff placement to your liking. Hand stitch the ends of each cuff into place with a few tacking stitches.

11. Press the collar so that it lies completely flat (it will resemble a butterfly shape). Tie the collar in a knot at the middle and adjust it to your preference to mimic the look of a bow. Place the bow over the gap between the 2 cuffs and adjust it to your liking. Sew it in place with some tacking stitches.

12. Press and steam lightly to get the shape nice and crisp. Pin the ribbon along the inside of the hat to cover the brim seam allowances neatly. Hand stitch into place, being sure to stitch only through the lining fabric. Wear and enjoy!

child's aviator

HAT SIZE: *Fits 1- to 2-year-old child (head circumference 18˝–20˝, measured just above the ears)*

Whether you choose to make a winter hat using fleece as the lining or an all-season cycling hat using cotton as the lining, your little aviator will look as sweet as can be in this gender-neutral cap. And it's reversible! The designer recycled a pair of big, ugly corduroy trousers and found the retro cotton print for the reverse side at the East Bay Depot for Creative Reuse, so scour the thrift stores for your materials, or buy from the bolt. Either way, this aviator is perfect for the toddler in your life.

Ivy Young has always been crafty, and along with sewing hats, she enjoys screen printing, making crochet sculpture, and knitting socks. Ivy started sewing in San Francisco just before her son Otis was born. Because she believes in sustainable lifestyles, Ivy intended to get out and ride her bike with her new baby as soon as possible, but she found a notable lack of child-sized cycling caps. With the help of her friend, May, she began experimenting with itty bitty pattern making and was soon selling her Wee Caps and Flappy Caps at local shops and on Etsy. Ivy is dedicated to selling sustainably made products using quality reclaimed materials. Ivy and Otis encourage all to ride safely, and do the best you can.

ARTIST: Ivy Young
Ivy and Otis
WEBSITES: etsy.com/shop/ivyandotis
ivyandotis.tumblr.com
facebook.com/pages/Ivy-and-
Otis/206304606077985

Materials and Supplies

Fabric A: ⅝ yard

Fabric B: ⅝ yard

Cutting

Template patterns are on pullout page P1. Enlarge patterns 200%.

Note: Label the wrong side of the shell triangles with numbers 1–6 for Fabric A and Fabric B. Mark a turning hole on the wrong side of shell piece 1. Mark the tie placement on the wrong side of the earflap pieces.

FABRIC A:

Cut 6 shells.

Cut 1 earflap.

Cut 1 brim.

Cut 2 ties (from Fabric A *or* Fabric B).

FABRIC B:

Cut 6 shells.

Cut 1 earflap.

Cut 1 brim.

Cut 2 ties (from Fabric A *or* Fabric B).

CONSTRUCTION

Note: Use a ¼˝ seam allowance unless otherwise noted.

Brim, ties, and earflaps

1. Place the brim pieces of Fabrics A and B right sides together. Pin and sew along the curved edge of the brim. Clip the curves.

2. Turn the brim right side out and press the seam. Set aside.

3. Fold each tie in half, with right sides together, along the long edge, and press. Sew the long edge.

4. Use a safety pin to turn each tie right side out. Knot an end of each tie and trim. Set aside.

Shells

5. Place the earflap pieces of Fabrics A and B right sides together. Pin along the curved edge of the earflap. Pin the ties in where marked. The ties should be between the 2 earflap pieces, with the raw edges sticking out about ¼˝.

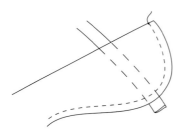

6. Sew along the curved seam of the earflap. Trim the excess from the ties and clip the curves. Turn right side out and press the seam flat.

1. Place shell pieces 1 and 2 of Fabric A right sides together. Starting ¼˝ down from the peak, stitch the right-hand side. Press the seam to the right.

2. Match shell pieces 2 and 3 right sides together and repeat Step 1. Continue with pieces 3 and 4, 4 and 5, and 5 and 6, each time making sure to begin the seam ¼˝ from the peak of the shell.

3. Finally, match shell pieces 1 and 6 right sides together and pin. To help match up the seams at the peak of the cap, lay the shell piece flat, allowing the seams to lie to the right all the way around the cap. Begin the final seam ½˝ from the peak on the seam opposite from pieces 1 and 6. (This should be pieces 3 and 4.) You will be sewing across the peak of the cap. To prevent puckering at the peak, make sure the cap is flat and that all the seams are lying in the same direction. Turn the shell right side out and inspect the peak to ensure that there are no puckers or holes. This is now called shell A.

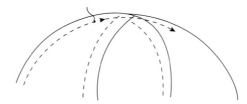

4. Repeat Steps 1–3 using Fabric B. This is now called shell B.

5. Nest shell A and shell B with right sides together. Pin the peaks together, and line up seams 3–4 on both shells 1–6 on both shells. Working your way around the base of the shells, ensure that the seams from shell A and shell B line up exactly. Pin each seam to check. If a seam does not match up, bring in the seam of the larger shell until the seams match. Do not skip this step.

6. Unpin and set aside.

Finishing

1. Topstitch the brim piece ⅛″ from the seam edge using contrasting or matching top-stitching thread. Topstitch again ¼″ from the first line, and again ¼″ from the second line.

2. Topstitch the earflap piece ⅛″ from the seam edge.

3. Topstitch along the right side of each seam of shells A and B, starting at the base and stopping when you reach the seam at the peak. The top-stitching lines will not match up at the peak.

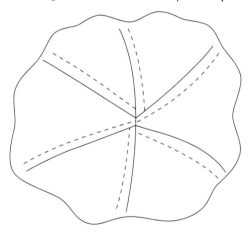

4. With right sides together, pin the peak of shell A to the peak of shell B, ensuring that the long seam lines up. Center the brim at shell seam 3–4, ensuring that Fabric A of the brim is facing shell A, and Fabric B of the brim is facing shell B. (The brim should be inside the 2 shells, with raw edges together.) Pin at the center of the brim through both shells.

5. Center the earflap piece in the same way, opposite the center of the brim, at shell seam 1–6. To do this, you will need to stuff the ties between the shell pieces. Do so in a way that ensures that the ties are not sewn into the base of the hat.

6. Pin around the base of the cap, leaving a turning hole where marked on piece 1. (The hole should be opposite the brim.) Sew around the raw edge with a ½″ seam allowance, starting and ending at the turning hole. You should not be able to see the brim, earflaps, or ties! Clip the curves and turn the cap right side out.

7. Press both sides of the seam up. Press under the raw edge of the turning hole to match the seam.

8. Starting at the turning hole, topstitch ⅛″ above the final seam all the way around the base of the hat. (This topstitching is also what closes the turning hole.)

juliet headband

SIZE: *Fits all*

This simple yet elegant headband combines some easy embroidery stitches with a strip of wool felt to create a subtle design that has just a blush of color. Customize the materials based on a color palate just right for the wearer. It's so easy to make and adds a charming hint of handmade to any outfit. A great project for beginners.

Sandie Zimmerman is quite the old-fashioned girl, which is probably the reason that embroidery and sewing by hand appeal to her. Her mom taught her to embroider when she was eight or nine years old. Sandie's mom taught her all the stitches, but the lazy daisy stitch was always her favorite. She practiced for hours and made hundreds, if not thousands, of lazy daisy stitches. Today, she embroiders freehand and most of her designs consist of patterns made from her favorite stitch, with some cross-stitch and running stitch mixed in. She has a love for forgotten things and old houses, and the soft, muted colors she uses reflect that love. She is at her most content when she has a needle in one hand, a piece of felt in the other, and a box of thread at her side.

ARTIST: Sandie Zimmerman

Materials and Supplies

Ivory wool felt: 1 piece at least 4˝ × 14˝

Fabric glue

Black elastic headband

DMC embroidery thread in 3 colors (Colors pictured: 3866, 3861, and 453)

Large needle, such as an embroidery or darning needle

Cutting

Template pattern is on page P2. Enlarge pattern 200%. From the ivory felt, cut 2 strips 2˝ × 14˝.

CONSTRUCTION

1. Draw the embroidery pattern from the template onto a strip of felt using a disappearing-ink marker.

2. Embroider the design on the felt according to the pattern.

3. Cut a black elastic headband in half.

4. Position the embroidered felt on top of the second piece of felt. Insert the ends of the cut headband ½˝ in, between the ends of the 2 pieces of felt. Using fabric glue, glue together the 2 pieces of felt with the ends of the headband inside.

5. When the glue is dry, cut ⅛˝ around the edges of the embroidery to create a scalloped effect.

6. Make a couple of stitches with DMC 3866 to secure the ends of the elastic headband to the felt.

stashBOOKS

fabric arts for a handmade lifestyle

If you're craving beautiful authenticity in a time of mass-production...Stash Books is for you. Stash Books is a line of how-to books celebrating fabric arts for a handmade lifestyle. Backed by C&T Publishing's solid reputation for quality, Stash Books will inspire you with contemporary designs, clear and simple instructions, and engaging photography.

www.stashbooks.com